Go in Action, A Hands-On Approach to Programming with Go

Learn Practical Go Programming Techniques for Developing Cutting-Edge Applications

Booker Blunt

Rafael Sanders

Miguel Farmer

Boozman Richard

Contents

How to Scan a Barcode to Get a Repository

1. **Install a QR/Barcode Scanner** - Ensure you have a barcode or QR code scanner app installed on your smartphone or use a built-in scanner in **GitHub, GitLab, or Bitbucket.**

2. **Open the Scanner** - Launch the scanner app and grant necessary camera permissions.

3. **Scan the Barcode** - Align the barcode within the scanning frame. The scanner will automatically detect and process it.

4. **Follow the Link** - The scanned result will display a **URL to the repository.** Tap the link to open it in your web browser or Git client.

5. **Clone the Repository** - Use **Git clone** with the provided URL to download the repository to your local machine.

Chapter 1: Understanding Go and Setting Up Your Development Environment

Introduction

Welcome to the world of Go programming! Whether you're new to programming or an experienced developer looking to expand your toolkit, Go offers a powerful and efficient way to build applications. Known for its simplicity and high performance, Go has become a favorite among startups and large enterprises alike. This chapter will introduce you to Go, guide you through setting up your development environment, and walk you through your first

"Hello, World!" program. By the end of this chapter, you'll have a solid foundation in Go, setting you up for success as you dive deeper into the language.

Why Go? The Growing Popularity of Go Programming

Go, also known as Golang, was developed by Google engineers Robert Griesemer, Rob Pike, and Ken Thompson in 2007 and released publicly in 2009. It was designed to address issues with existing programming languages such as C++ and Java, focusing on simplicity, speed, and ease of use. Go aims to be a language that's easy to learn, even for beginners, while also providing advanced features for professional developers.

In today's rapidly evolving tech landscape, Go has become a go-to language for a wide range of applications. From web servers and APIs to machine learning and cloud computing, Go's versatility and robustness have made it a strong contender in industries ranging from healthcare to finance. But what exactly makes Go so attractive?

Key Reasons for Go's Popularity

- **Simplicity and Efficiency:** Go's syntax is clean and easy to understand, with a minimalistic approach to programming. This makes it perfect for both beginners and experienced developers who want to write efficient code quickly.

- **High Performance:** Go is a compiled language, meaning it directly converts your code into machine-readable code. This results in faster execution times compared to interpreted languages.

- **Concurrency Made Easy:** Go's built-in support for concurrency (via goroutines and channels) makes it easier to write efficient, multi-threaded applications.
- **Wide Use in Modern Development:** Companies like Uber, Dropbox, and Docker rely on Go for their core infrastructure because it can handle high performance and scalability requirements.
- **Open Source with a Strong Community:** Go is open-source, and its active community provides resources, frameworks, and libraries to extend its capabilities.

Now that you have an idea of why Go is so popular, let's dive into how you can get started with it!

Core Concepts and Theory

Before diving into writing code, it's essential to understand the key concepts that make Go unique. This section covers the foundational elements of Go, such as its history, syntax, data types, and more. By understanding these core ideas, you'll have a clearer grasp of how Go works and why it's such a powerful tool for developers.

1. The Go Language: A Quick Overview

Go is a statically typed, compiled programming language, which means that the types of variables are explicitly declared, and the source code is compiled directly into machine code before it runs. This allows for faster execution and better performance, making Go ideal for large-scale applications.

- **Statically Typed**: Variables must be declared with a type (such as int, string, etc.), and the compiler checks for type errors at compile-time.
- **Compiled**: Go is compiled into machine code, so you don't need an interpreter or virtual machine to run your programs. This is why Go applications can be very fast.
- **Concurrent**: One of Go's standout features is its ability to handle multiple tasks concurrently, using goroutines and channels. This makes Go a great choice for building scalable applications, like web servers or distributed systems.

2. Key Features of Go

- **Simplicity**: Go follows the principle of "keep it simple." Its syntax is designed to be easy to read and write, with no complex inheritance hierarchies or generic types (though generics have been introduced in Go 1.18).

- **Garbage Collection**: Go has built-in garbage collection, which automatically manages memory, freeing up space that is no longer needed.
- **Standard Library**: Go comes with an extensive standard library that provides built-in tools for handling things like file I/O, networking, and concurrency. This reduces the need for third-party libraries and tools.
- **Cross-Platform**: Go supports multiple operating systems, allowing developers to write code that can run on Windows, macOS, and Linux with minimal changes.

3. How Go Handles Concurrency

Concurrency refers to the ability of a program to run multiple tasks at the same time. Go makes it easy to write concurrent programs, thanks to goroutines and channels:

- **Goroutines:** These are lightweight, concurrent functions in Go that can run simultaneously. Think of them like threads in other programming languages but are more memory-efficient.
- **Channels:** Channels allow goroutines to communicate with each other. They are a core part of Go's concurrency model and provide a safe way to share data between goroutines.

4. Go's Syntax: The Basics

Go's syntax is simple and follows a consistent set of rules. Below are some fundamental syntax concepts in Go:

- **Variables**: Go uses var to declare variables, and types are specified after the variable name. For example:

```go
go

var x int = 5
```

- **Functions**: Functions in Go are declared with the func keyword, followed by the function name, parameters, and return type. Here's an example:

```go
go

func greet(name string) string {
    return "Hello, " + name
}
```

- **Loops and Conditionals**: Go supports traditional loops (for) and conditionals (if and switch).

Tools and Setup

Now that we've covered the key concepts behind Go, it's time to get your development environment set up. In this section, we'll guide you through the steps needed to install Go on your machine and choose the best Integrated Development Environment (IDE) to start coding.

1. Installing Go

To start programming in Go, you need to install it on your system. Here's how you can do it on Windows, macOS, and Linux.

Windows:

1. Download the latest version of Go from the official website.
2. Run the installer and follow the on-screen instructions.
3. After installation, open a command prompt and type go version to verify the installation.

macOS:

1. Download the latest version of Go from the official website.
2. Open the .pkg file and follow the installation instructions.
3. After installation, open Terminal and type go version to check the installation.

Linux:

1. Open the terminal and run the following commands:

```bash
sudo apt update
sudo apt install golang-go
```

2. Verify the installation by typing go version in the terminal.

Setting the Go Path: Go uses the GOPATH environment variable to locate your Go workspace. This path points to the directory where your Go projects are stored. You can set it like this:

Windows:

1. Right-click on “My Computer” > Properties > Advanced system settings > Environment Variables.

2. Add a new environment variable GOPATH and set the path to your workspace (e.g., C:\Users\YourName\go).

macOS/Linux:

1. Open .bash_profile or .zshrc in your home directory.
2. Add the line export GOPATH=$HOME/go and save the file.
3. Run source ~/.bash_profile (or source ~/.zshrc for zsh).

2. IDE and Tools Setup

While you can use any text editor to write Go code, it's helpful to use an IDE or code editor that supports Go syntax and has built-in tools for debugging and running your code. Two of the most popular choices are:

- **VS Code**:
  1. Download and install VS Code.
  2. Install the Go extension for VS Code by going to Extensions and searching for "Go".
  3. Set up the Go tools in VS Code, which will allow you to format code, run tests, and manage packages.
- **GoLand**: GoLand is a full-featured IDE specifically designed for Go. If you're looking for a more professional experience, GoLand offers advanced features like code completion, refactoring, and version control integration.

3. Go's Built-In Tools: go run, go build, and go fmt

Go comes with several built-in tools that make it easier to develop, test, and maintain your programs. Let's take a look at three important commands:

- **go run**: This command allows you to run Go programs directly from the command line. It compiles and executes the Go code in one step.

```
bash

go run main.go
```

- **go build**: This command compiles your Go code into an executable file.

```
bash

go build main.go
```

- **go fmt:** This tool automatically formats your Go code according to Go's style guidelines.

```bash
go fmt main.go
```

Hands-on Examples & Projects

Now that your environment is set up, let's dive into writing some code! In this section, we'll walk you through a few hands-on examples to help you get comfortable with Go's syntax and structure.

First Go Program: "Hello, World!"

1. Create a new file named main.go in your project directory.
2. Type the following code:

```go
```

```go
package main

import "fmt"

func main() {
    fmt.Println("Hello, World!")
}
```

3. Save the file and run it using the following command:

```bash
bash

go run main.go
```

4. The output should be:

```
Hello, World!
```

This simple program demonstrates how to structure a Go program, including the package main, the import statement, and the main() function, which is the entry point of every Go program.

Building a Simple Calculator

Let's build a basic calculator that takes user input and performs simple arithmetic operations. This will help you understand how to work with user input, variables, and control structures in Go.

```
go

package main

import "fmt"

func main() {
    var num1, num2, result float64
    var operator string

    fmt.Print("Enter first number: ")
    fmt.Scanln(&num1)

    fmt.Print("Enter operator (+, -, *,
/): ")
    fmt.Scanln(&operator)

    fmt.Print("Enter second number: ")
```

```
    fmt.Scanln(&num2)

    switch operator {
    case "+":
        result = num1 + num2
    case "-":
        result = num1 - num2
    case "*":
        result = num1 * num2
    case "/":
        if num2 != 0 {
            result = num1 / num2
        } else {
            fmt.Println("Error:
Division by zero")
            return
        }
    default:
        fmt.Println("Invalid operator")
        return
    }

    fmt.Printf("The result of %.2f %s
%.2f = %.2f\n", num1, operator, num2,
result)
```

}

Run this code and input different numbers and operators to see how it works.

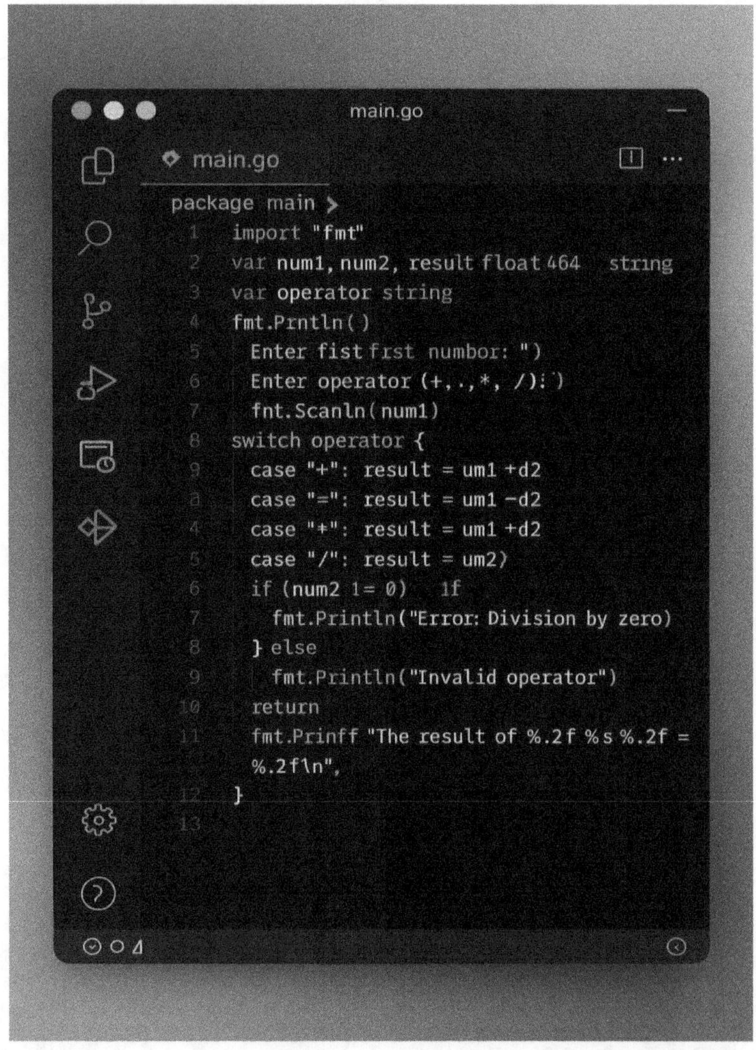

main.go
main.go
package main >
import "fmt"
var num1, num2, result float 464 string
var operator string
fmt.Prntln( )
Enter fist frst numbor: ")
Enter operator (+, ., *, /):')
fnt.Scanln(num1)
switch operator {
case "+": result = um1 +d2
case "=": result = um1 -d2
case "+": result = um1 +d2
case "/": result = um2)
if (num2 1= 0) 1f
fmt.Println("Error: Division by zero)
} else
fmt.Println("Invalid operator")
return
fmt.Prinff "The result of %.2f %s %.2f =
%.2f\n",
}

Advanced Techniques & Optimization

As you grow more comfortable with Go, you'll want to explore advanced topics such as optimization techniques, Go's concurrency model, and error handling. Understanding how Go handles memory management, CPU usage, and error handling can help you write more efficient and maintainable code.

In the next chapter, we will dive into concurrency and goroutines—one of Go's most powerful features.

Troubleshooting and Problem-Solving

As with any programming language, you'll inevitably encounter challenges while working with Go. Here are some common issues and how to troubleshoot them:

- **Syntax Errors**: These occur when Go encounters code that doesn't follow the correct syntax. For example, missing semicolons or mismatched parentheses will generate syntax errors.
- **Type Errors:** Go is strongly typed, so type mismatches (e.g., trying to assign a string to an integer variable) will result in compilation errors.
- **Runtime Errors**: These happen while the program is running. For example, division by zero or null pointer dereferencing can cause crashes.

We'll explore how to handle these errors in the next chapters.

Conclusion & Next Steps

Congratulations! You've now set up your Go development environment, written your first Go program, and gained a basic understanding of the language's core concepts. In the next chapter, we will dive deeper into Go's powerful concurrency model and show you how to write concurrent programs using goroutines and channels.

By continuing with this book, you'll learn how to leverage Go's strengths to build real-world applications. The possibilities are endless, and with Go's simplicity and performance, you'll be ready to tackle even the most complex projects.

Chapter 2: Diving into Go Syntax and Data Structures

Introduction

Welcome to Chapter 2! Now that you've gotten your development environment set up, it's time to dive into the heart of Go programming–the syntax and data structures. This chapter will take you through the foundational aspects of Go, including how to declare and use variables, understand Go's strong typing system, and work with data structures like arrays, slices, and maps. Along the way, we'll break down essential control structures, such as loops and conditionals, and walk through hands-on projects to reinforce these concepts.

If you’re new to programming or transitioning from another language, this chapter will equip you with the skills to write clean, efficient Go code. Whether you're building web applications, data processors, or systems software, understanding Go’s syntax and data structures is key to leveraging the full power of the language.

What You’ll Learn in This Chapter:

- **Variables, Constants, and Types**: Learn how to declare and use variables, constants, and data types in Go.
- **Control Structures**: Master the if/else, switch, and looping constructs in Go.
- **Arrays and Slices**: Understand the difference between arrays and slices and learn when to use each.
- **Maps**: Learn how to work with key-value pairs in Go using maps.

- **Hands-on Project:** Build a simple calculator application that demonstrates the use of variables, loops, and basic arithmetic.

Key Concepts and Terminology

- **Variables:** Containers for storing data that can change.
- **Constants:** Immutable values that don't change during the program's execution.
- **Types:** Defines the kind of data a variable can hold (e.g., integers, floats, strings).
- **Control Structures:** Direct how the program makes decisions and repeats actions.
- **Arrays and Slices:** Collections of elements.
- **Maps:** Key-value data structure that stores associations between keys and values.

Core Concepts and Theory

To understand Go deeply, it's crucial to get comfortable with its syntax and data types. In this section, we'll break down Go's core concepts, providing clear explanations and examples for each.

1. Variables, Constants, and Types

Declaring Variables in Go

In Go, variables must be declared before they are used. Go's type system requires that every variable has a specific type, whether it's an integer, string, or boolean.

Here's how you declare variables in Go:

```go
var age int = 30
var name string = "John Doe"
```

In the example above:

- age is an integer (int), and name is a string (string).

Short Variable Declaration

Go offers a shorthand for declaring and initializing variables within functions. Instead of writing var age int = 30, you can use :=:

```go
age := 30
name := "John Doe"
```

This shorthand automatically infers the type of the variable based on the assigned value.

Constants

A constant in Go is a value that cannot be changed after it's declared. Constants are defined using the const keyword:

```go
```

```
const Pi = 3.14159
```

Once defined, Pi cannot be modified.

Understanding Go's Strong Type System

Go's strong type system means you must specify the data type for variables and constants. This avoids bugs that arise from unexpected type conversions. For example:

```go
var age int = 25
// age = "twenty five" // This would result in a compile-time error
```

Go enforces type safety, ensuring that a variable declared as an integer cannot be assigned a string or float unless explicitly cast.

Working with Different Types

Go supports a variety of basic types:

- **Integers**: int, int8, int16, int32, int64, uint, uint8, uint16, uint32, uint64
- **Floating-Point Numbers**: float32, float64
- **Booleans**: bool
- **Strings**: string

Example:

```go
var a int = 5
var b float64 = 3.14
var c bool = true
var d string = "Hello, Go!"
```

---

2. Control Structures

Control structures allow you to control the flow of your program based on conditions or to repeat certain actions. Go's main control structures are if/else, switch, and loops.

If/Else Statements

Go uses if and else to conditionally execute code based on boolean expressions.

```go
age := 18
if age >= 18 {
    fmt.Println("You are an adult.")
} else {
    fmt.Println("You are a minor.")
}
```

Switch Statements

Go's switch is similar to if/else but is often more concise when there are multiple conditions to check.

```go
day := "Monday"
switch day {
case "Monday":
```

```
    fmt.Println("Start of the work
week.")
case "Saturday", "Sunday":
    fmt.Println("Weekend!")
default:
    fmt.Println("Midweek days.")
}
```

Loops

Go has a single loop construct: the for loop. It can function as a traditional for loop, a while loop, or an infinite loop.

Traditional for loop:

```
go

for i := 0; i < 5; i++ {
    fmt.Println(i)
}
```

While loop (by omitting initialization and post statements):

```
go
```

```
i := 0
for i < 5 {
    fmt.Println(i)
    i++
}
```

Infinite loop:

```go
for {
    fmt.Println("This will run
forever!")
}
```

Breaking and Continuing Loops

Go allows you to control the flow within loops using break and continue.

- **break**: Exits the loop immediately.

```go
for i := 0; i < 10; i++ {
    if i == 5 {
        break
    }
```

```
    fmt.Println(i)
}
```

- **continue**: Skips the current iteration and moves to the next one.

```go
for i := 0; i < 10; i++ {
    if i%2 == 0 {
        continue
    }
    fmt.Println(i) // Prints only odd
numbers
}
```

---

3. Arrays and Slices

Arrays and slices are both used to store collections of data in Go, but they differ significantly in terms of flexibility and usage.

Arrays

An array is a fixed-length sequence of elements of the same type. Once you define the length of an array, it cannot change.

go

```
var numbers [5]int
numbers[0] = 10
numbers[1] = 20
fmt.Println(numbers) // Output: [10 20
0 0 0]
```

Slices

A slice is a more flexible and powerful construct in Go. Unlike arrays, slices are dynamically sized, and their size can change as elements are added or removed.

go

```
numbers := []int{10, 20, 30}
numbers = append(numbers, 40)
fmt.Println(numbers) // Output: [10 20
30 40]
```

Best Practices:

- Use slices when you need flexibility in the size of the collection.
- Use arrays when the size of the collection is fixed and known ahead of time.

---

4. Maps

Maps are Go's built-in associative data structures that store key-value pairs.

Creating and Modifying Maps

To create a map, you use the make function or a map literal. Here's an example of creating a map with string keys and integer values:

```go
ages := make(map[string]int)
ages["Alice"] = 25
ages["Bob"] = 30
```

```
fmt.Println(ages) // Output:
map[Alice:25 Bob:30]
```

You can also initialize a map with values directly:

```go
ages := map[string]int{
    "Alice": 25,
    "Bob":   30,
}
```

Accessing and Modifying Maps

Maps allow you to access values using the key and also check if the key exists.

```go
age, exists := ages["Alice"]
if exists {
    fmt.Println("Alice's age:", age)
} else {
    fmt.Println("Alice not found")
}
```

Best Practices for Using Maps

- Maps are efficient for lookups, but the order of keys is not guaranteed.
- When using maps in concurrent programs, make sure to use synchronization primitives (like channels or sync.Mutex) to avoid race conditions.

Hands-On Example: Building a Simple Calculator

In this section, we will apply what we've learned so far by building a simple calculator in Go that performs basic arithmetic operations. This project will involve using variables, loops, conditionals, and functions.

Step 1: Define the Calculator Function

We'll start by creating a simple calculator that can add, subtract, multiply, and divide two numbers.

```
go

package main

import "fmt"

func main() {
    var num1, num2 float64
    var operator string

    fmt.Print("Enter first number: ")
    fmt.Scanln(&num1)

    fmt.Print("Enter operator (+, -, *,
/): ")
    fmt.Scanln(&operator)

    fmt.Print("Enter second number: ")
    fmt.Scanln(&num2)
```

```
    var result float64
    switch operator {
    case "+":
        result = num1 + num2
    case "-":
        result = num1 - num2
    case "*":
        result = num1 * num2
    case "/":
        if num2 != 0 {
            result = num1 / num2
        } else {
            fmt.Println("Error:
Division by zero is not allowed.")
            return
        }
    default:
        fmt.Println("Invalid
operator!")
        return
    }

    fmt.Printf("Result: %.2f %s %.2f =
%.2f\n", num1, operator, num2, result)
```

}

calculator.go

OPEN EDITORS

ccalculator.go

```
package main
import 'fmt"

func main() {
  var num1,num flot64
  var operator string
  fmt.Print("Enter first number: ")
  fmt.Scanln("€ operator (+,-,+):):
  fmt.Println("Enter second number:
  result num2)
  switch operator {
   case "+":
   case "-"= num1 + num2
   case "*"= num1 - num2
   if (num2 == 0) if num2
     result = num1 / num2
     return
   default: ('Invalid operator!")
   return
  fmt.Pritff("Result: 2.2f sx 3.20f
  3.2f =,num1, operator, nu2,
  result)
}
```

O Go

Step 2: Run the Calculator

Run the code by entering values for the numbers and operator, and the program will output the result.

Advanced Techniques & Optimization

As you become more comfortable with Go, you'll need to learn how to optimize your code for performance. In this section, we'll discuss some best practices for writing efficient Go code, particularly when working with arrays, slices, and maps. We'll also look into how to handle larger datasets and optimize memory usage.

Troubleshooting and Problem-Solving

While working with Go, you may encounter some common issues, such as type mismatches or runtime errors. Here are some common problems and how to troubleshoot them:

- **Type Mismatches**: Go is a strongly typed language, so you'll get compile-time errors if you try to assign a variable of one type to a variable of another type.
- **Index Out of Range**: When working with arrays or slices, make sure you're not accessing an index that's out of bounds.

Conclusion & Next Steps

By the end of this chapter, you should have a solid understanding of Go's syntax, control structures, and data types. You've also completed your first hands-on project—a calculator that uses loops, conditionals, and basic arithmetic operations.

In the next chapter, we'll dive deeper into Go's more advanced features, such as error handling and Go's unique concurrency model, which will allow you to write more efficient, parallel applications.

Chapter 3: Functions and Error Handling

Introduction

In Go, functions are one of the core building blocks of your programs. A good understanding of how to define and use functions will help you structure your code more efficiently, improve readability, and ultimately make you a better Go developer. This chapter dives deep into functions in Go, showing you how to define functions, pass parameters, and even handle multiple return values—a unique feature of Go. Moreover, we'll explore error handling, which is critical in ensuring that your Go applications behave reliably, even when things go wrong.

Whether you're building small utilities or large, production-ready systems, understanding how to handle errors and design functions properly is essential. Go emphasizes simplicity and clarity, which reflects in its approach to error handling. This chapter will equip you with the knowledge to write well-structured functions, gracefully handle errors, and create applications that are both effective and easy to debug.

What You'll Learn in This Chapter:

- **Defining Functions**: Learn how to declare functions, use parameters, and define return types.
- **Named and Anonymous Functions**: Understand the difference and when to use each type of function.
- **Multiple Return Values**: Explore Go's unique ability to return multiple values, including how to return both a result and an error.

- **Error Handling:** Understand the importance of error handling in Go, how to create custom errors, and best practices for managing error flow in your programs.
- **Hands-On Project:** Build a basic file manager that reads, writes, and deletes files while properly handling errors.

By the end of this chapter, you'll not only have a strong grasp of Go's function system but also be equipped to write more reliable and resilient applications by using proper error handling techniques.

Core Concepts and Theory

1. Defining Functions in Go

A function in Go is a block of code that can be executed when it is called. Functions allow you to reuse code and structure your programs in a modular way. Here, we'll walk through how to define functions, use parameters, and specify return types in Go.

Function Declaration

In Go, you define a function using the func keyword, followed by the function name, parameters (if any), and return types (if any). Here's a simple example:

```
go

package main

import "fmt"

// Function that adds two numbers and
returns the result
func add(a int, b int) int {
    return a + b
}
```

```
func main() {
    result := add(5, 3)
    fmt.Println("The sum is:", result)
// Output: The sum is: 8
}
```

In the above example:

- add is the function name.
- (a int, b int) specifies the parameters, with their respective types (int).
- The return type int indicates that the function returns an integer value.

Named vs. Anonymous Functions

Go allows you to define both **named** and **anonymous** functions.

Named Functions

These are the functions you've seen in the previous example. They are defined with a name, allowing you to call them repeatedly in different parts of your program.

Anonymous Functions

These are functions that do not have a name. They are typically used when you need a function for a short-term purpose, such as passing it as a parameter to another function.

```go
go

package main

import "fmt"

func main() {
    // Anonymous function assigned to a
variable
    greet := func(name string) {
        fmt.Println("Hello,", name)
    }

    // Calling the anonymous function
```

```
    greet("Alice") // Output: Hello,
Alice
}
```

Anonymous functions are useful when you need a quick function, such as in callbacks or when passing functions as parameters.

2. Parameters and Return Types

Go functions allow you to pass data to and from them using parameters and return values. Let's explore both of these concepts in more detail.

Multiple Parameters

Go allows you to pass multiple parameters to a function. You can either declare each parameter with its type or group multiple parameters of the same type together:

```
go

func printDetails(name string, age int)
{
    fmt.Println("Name:", name)
```

```
    fmt.Println("Age:", age)
}
```

Alternatively, for multiple parameters of the same type:

```go

func sum(a, b, c int) int {
    return a + b + c
}
```

Multiple Return Values

One of Go's most distinctive features is the ability to return multiple values from a function. This is especially useful for returning both a result and an error, which is common in Go's approach to error handling.

```go

func divide(a, b int) (int, error) {
    if b == 0 {
        return 0, fmt.Errorf("division
by zero")
    }
```

```
    return a / b, nil
}

func main() {
    result, err := divide(10, 2)
    if err != nil {
        fmt.Println("Error:", err)
    } else {
        fmt.Println("Result:", result)
// Output: Result: 5
    }
}
```

In this example:

- The function divide returns two values: the result of the division and an error.
- If division by zero is attempted, the function returns an error using Go's fmt.Errorf function.
- The calling function can then handle the error appropriately.

Named Return Values

Go also allows you to define named return values for functions. This can help make the function's behavior clearer and eliminate the need to explicitly return values at the end of the function.

```
go

func multiply(a, b int) (result int) {
    result = a * b
    return // No need to explicitly
return result
}
```

3. Error Handling in Go

In Go, error handling is explicit and simple. Unlike languages that use exceptions, Go uses a unique approach where functions that can fail return an error value as the last return value. The calling code is then responsible for checking the error and handling it appropriately.

The Error Type

Go has a built-in error type, which is an interface that holds an error message:

```go
type error interface {
    Error() string
}
```

You can create custom errors using fmt.Errorf or implement your own error types by defining a custom struct and implementing the Error() method.

Error Handling Best Practices

- **Always Check for Errors:** In Go, it's important to always check for errors after calling functions that return them. If you fail to check errors, your program might behave unexpectedly.

```go
result, err := divide(10, 0)
if err != nil {
    fmt.Println("Error:", err)
} else {
    fmt.Println("Result:", result)
}
```

- **Handling Errors Gracefully:** When an error occurs, you should handle it in a way that ensures your program remains stable. For instance, if a file operation fails, provide a helpful error message and prevent the program from crashing.

```go
file, err := os.Open("example.txt")
if err != nil {
    log.Fatalf("Error opening file:
%v", err)
}
```

- **Creating Custom Errors:** You can create more specific error messages using fmt.Errorf or define custom error types.

```go
go

type MyError struct {
    Code    int
    Message string
}

func (e *MyError) Error() string {
    return fmt.Sprintf("Code %d: %s",
e.Code, e.Message)
}

func generateError() error {
    return &MyError{Code: 404, Message:
"Not Found"}
}
```

Tools and Setup

To follow along with the hands-on examples and projects in this chapter, you'll need a Go development environment set up. If you haven't already installed Go, refer back to Chapter 1 for detailed instructions on installing Go on Windows, macOS, or Linux.

Here's a quick rundown of the tools and libraries we'll use in this chapter:

- **Go Programming Language**: You'll need Go installed to run the examples and projects. Visit Go's official site to get started.
- **Text Editor or IDE**: Use any text editor or IDE that supports Go syntax. Some popular choices are Visual Studio Code with the Go plugin or GoLand (a specialized Go IDE).
- **Standard Library**: We'll use Go's built-in packages such as fmt, os, and log for

various functionalities. No additional libraries are needed.

Hands-On Examples & Projects

Creating a Basic File Manager

In this section, we'll create a basic file manager application. The application will perform three file operations—reading, writing, and deleting files—and handle any errors that arise during these operations.

Step 1: Define Functions for File Operations

We'll start by writing functions to perform basic file operations. Each function will return an error if the operation fails.

```go
go

package main
```

```
import (
    "fmt"
    "io/ioutil"
    "os"
)

func writeFile(filename, content
string) error {
    return ioutil.WriteFile(filename,
[]byte(content), 0644)
}

func readFile(filename string) (string,
error) {
    content, err :=
ioutil.ReadFile(filename)
    if err != nil {
        return "", err
    }
    return string(content), nil
}

func deleteFile(filename string) error
{
```

```
    return os.Remove(filename)
}

func main() {
    // Example usage of the file
manager functions
    err := writeFile("example.txt",
"Hello, Go!")
    if err != nil {
        fmt.Println("Error writing
file:", err)
        return
    }

    content, err :=
readFile("example.txt")
    if err != nil {
        fmt.Println("Error reading
file:", err)
        return
    }
    fmt.Println("File content:",
content)

    err = deleteFile("example.txt")
```

```
    if err != nil {
        fmt.Println("Error deleting
file:", err)
        return
    }

    fmt.Println("File deleted
successfully")
}
```

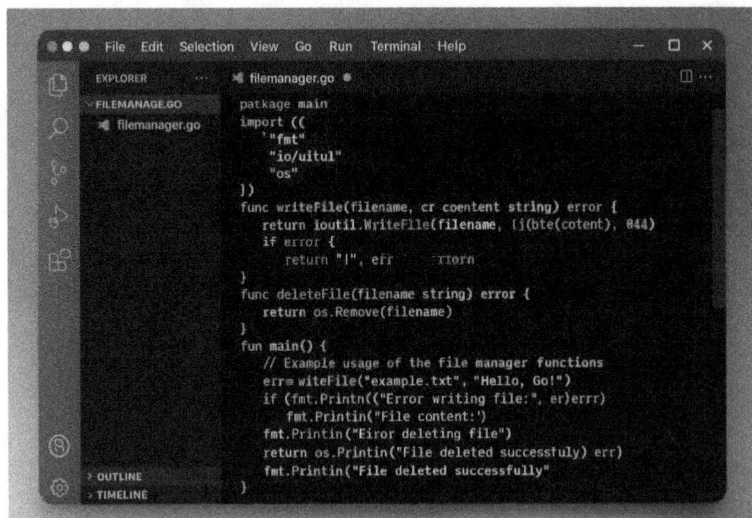

Step 2: Error Handling in File Operations

Notice that each function returns an error. In the main function, we check for errors after each file operation and handle them accordingly. If an error occurs, it's logged, and further operations are skipped.

Advanced Techniques & Optimization

Optimizing Error Handling

In Go, handling errors consistently across your program is crucial. One approach is to use custom error types for more structured and detailed error reporting. Additionally, managing large applications with extensive error handling requires establishing clear patterns for error management.

Performance Considerations

When working with file operations, it's essential to handle large files efficiently. Techniques such as buffered reading and writing can help improve performance, especially when dealing with I/O-bound tasks.

Troubleshooting and Problem-Solving

Common Issues and Fixes

- **File Not Found**: If you try to read a file that doesn't exist, Go will return an error. Always check if a file exists before trying to read it.
- **Permission Errors**: Ensure your program has the necessary permissions to read, write, or delete files in the directory.

Conclusion & Next Steps

Congratulations on completing this chapter! You've learned how to define functions, handle errors, and use Go's powerful error handling mechanisms to build more resilient applications. By implementing best practices for function design and error handling, you can ensure that your programs are not only functional but also maintainable and scalable.

In the next chapter, we'll explore Go's concurrency model, including how to use goroutines and channels to write highly concurrent applications. Get ready to dive deeper into Go's unique features!

Chapter 4: Working with Go's Concurrency Model

Introduction

Concurrency is one of the most powerful and distinctive features of Go. If you've ever worked with a program that performs multiple tasks simultaneously–whether it's handling multiple user requests on a web server or processing large datasets–concurrency is likely involved. Concurrency allows you to execute tasks in parallel, maximizing the efficiency of your application and improving its overall performance.

Go provides an elegant solution to concurrency with goroutines, channels, and the select statement. Understanding how to leverage these features is essential for writing efficient, scalable applications. Whether you're building a simple command-line tool or a complex web application, Go's concurrency model enables you to manage multiple tasks efficiently and safely.

In this chapter, we'll dive deep into the key components of Go's concurrency model:

- **Goroutines**: Lightweight threads of execution that allow tasks to run concurrently.
- **Channels**: The communication medium for passing data between goroutines.
- **Select Statement**: A tool for handling multiple channels simultaneously.

We'll also build a practical, hands-on project: a web scraper that fetches data from multiple web pages concurrently, processes it, and presents the results in a user-friendly format. By the end of this chapter, you will not only understand the theory behind Go's concurrency model but also how to apply it to real-world tasks.

Core Concepts and Theory

1. Goroutines: Introduction and Use Cases

A **goroutine** is Go's way of handling concurrency. They are lightweight, efficient threads of execution that allow your program to perform tasks concurrently with minimal overhead. Unlike traditional threads in other programming languages, goroutines are extremely lightweight and can be created in large quantities without using significant memory.

Creating and Managing Goroutines

To create a goroutine, you use the go keyword followed by a function call. This tells Go to run the function in a separate goroutine, allowing your program to continue executing the next statements concurrently.

Example:

```
go

package main

import "fmt"

func sayHello() {
    fmt.Println("Hello, World!")
}

func main() {
    go sayHello() // Start sayHello()
in a new goroutine
    fmt.Println("This runs concurrently
with sayHello()")
}
```

Here's what happens:

- The main function starts executing.

- The go sayHello() statement starts a new goroutine for sayHello.
- The main function prints its message and exits.
- The sayHello goroutine runs concurrently, and you may or may not see it execute before the program ends.

However, when running concurrent operations, there's no guarantee that the goroutines will finish in any specific order. This brings us to the next key concept: **channels**.

---

2. Channels: Communication Between Goroutines

Channels are the primary way goroutines communicate with each other. They allow you to safely send and receive data between goroutines, enabling synchronization and data passing in concurrent programs.

Creating and Using Channels

To create a channel in Go, you use the make function. Channels can be typed, meaning you specify the type of data that will be passed through the channel.

```
go

package main

import "fmt"

func sendData(ch chan string) {
    ch <- "Hello from goroutine"
}

func main() {
    ch := make(chan string) // Create a
channel of type string
```

```
    go sendData(ch) // Start a
goroutine to send data through the
channel

    msg := <-ch // Receive data from
the channel
    fmt.Println(msg) // Output: Hello
from goroutine
}
```

In this example:

- A goroutine is started with the go sendData(ch) statement.
- Inside the sendData function, the string "Hello from goroutine" is sent through the channel.
- In the main function, the channel is received with <-ch, and the value is printed.

Buffered vs. Unbuffered Channels

Channels in Go can be either **buffered** or **unbuffered**.

- **Unbuffered channels**: A channel that has no internal buffer. Data can only be sent and received when both the sender and receiver are ready.
- **Buffered channels**: A channel with a specified capacity. Data can be sent to the channel without being immediately received, as long as there is space in the buffer.

Example of a buffered channel:

```
go

ch := make(chan string, 2) // Buffered
channel with capacity 2
ch <- "first"  // Data is sent
ch <- "second" // Data is sent
fmt.Println(<-ch) // Output: first
fmt.Println(<-ch) // Output: second
```

Channel Synchronization

Channels are synchronized by default, meaning that only one goroutine can access the channel at a time. This synchronization makes it easy to coordinate goroutines and avoid race conditions, which can occur when multiple goroutines try to access shared data simultaneously.

---

3. The Select Statement: Handling Multiple Channels

The select statement in Go allows you to wait on multiple channels simultaneously. It is similar to switch, but instead of comparing values, it waits for communication on channels.

Using Select to Wait on Channels

When using select, your program can listen to multiple channels and react when data is available on one of them. Here's an example of a basic select statement:

```go
go

package main

import "fmt"

func main() {
	ch1 := make(chan string)
	ch2 := make(chan string)

	go func() {
		ch1 <- "Data from ch1"
	}()

	go func() {
		ch2 <- "Data from ch2"
	}()

	select {
	case msg1 := <-ch1:
		fmt.Println("Received:", msg1)
	case msg2 := <-ch2:
```

```
            fmt.Println("Received:", msg2)
        }
}
```

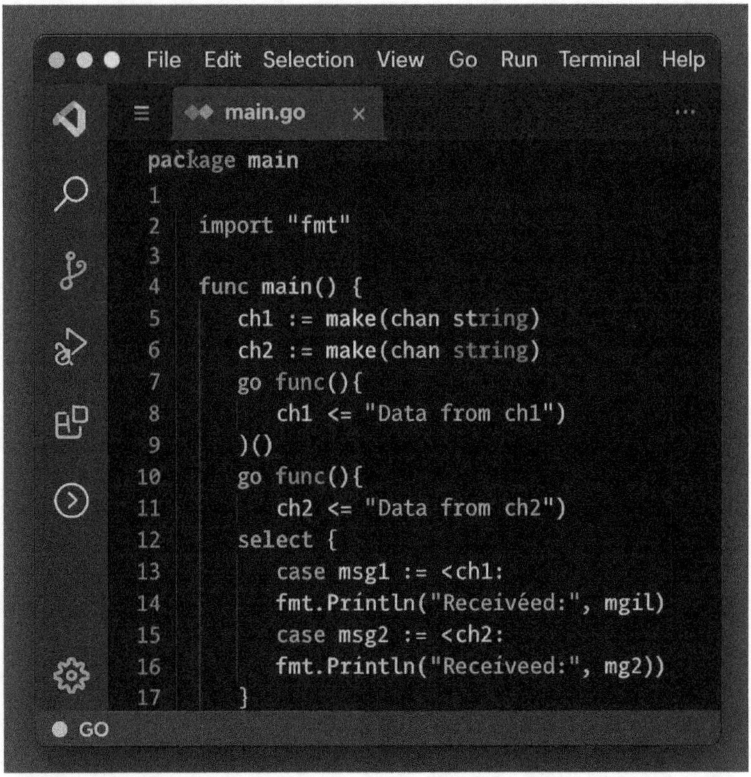

```
File Edit Selection View Go Run Terminal Help
main.go
package main

import "fmt"

func main() {
    ch1 := make(chan string)
    ch2 := make(chan string)
    go func(){
        ch1 <= "Data from ch1")
    )()
    go func(){
        ch2 <= "Data from ch2")
    select {
        case msg1 := <ch1:
        fmt.Println("Receivéed:", mgil)
        case msg2 := <ch2:
        fmt.Println("Receiveed:", mg2))
    }
GO
```

In this example:

- The program creates two channels (ch1 and ch2).
- Two goroutines send data to these channels concurrently.

- The select statement listens to both channels and prints the message from whichever channel is ready first.

Multiple Channels and Timeouts

The select statement is especially useful when you need to handle multiple channels and even implement timeouts. You can use a default case to handle situations when none of the channels are ready, or set a timeout to ensure that your program doesn't block indefinitely.

Example of a timeout:

```go
go

select {
case msg := <-ch1:
    fmt.Println("Received:", msg)
case <-time.After(3 * time.Second):
    fmt.Println("Timeout")
}
```

In this case, if no data is received from ch1 within 3 seconds, the program prints "Timeout".

Tools and Setup

To get started with concurrency in Go, you'll need:

- **Go installed**: Make sure you have Go installed on your system. If not, you can download it from the official Go website.
- **IDE or Text Editor:** While you can use any text editor, IDEs like **Visual Studio Code** with the Go extension or **GoLand** provide excellent support for Go development, including features like auto-completion and debugging.

Setting Up Go for Concurrency

1. **Install Go**: Follow the installation steps from Chapter 1.

2. **Set up your IDE**: Install the Go plugin for Visual Studio Code or GoLand for an enhanced development experience.

3. **Run the Examples**: Once you have your environment set up, you can the examples from this chapter and start experimenting with goroutines, channels, and the select statement.

Hands-on Examples & Projects

Web Scraper Project: Fetching Data Concurrently

In this section, we'll build a simple **web scraper** that fetches data from multiple web pages concurrently using Go's goroutines and channels.

Step 1: Define the Scraper Function

We'll begin by defining a function that fetches the content of a web page.

```
go

package main

import (
    "fmt"
    "net/http"
    "io/ioutil"
)

func fetchURL(url string, ch chan<-
string) {
    resp, err := http.Get(url)
    if err != nil {
        ch <- fmt.Sprintf("Error
fetching %s: %v", url, err)
        return
    }
    defer resp.Body.Close()
```

```
    body, err :=
ioutil.ReadAll(resp.Body)
    if err != nil {
        ch <- fmt.Sprintf("Error
reading body for %s: %v", url, err)
        return
    }
    ch <- fmt.Sprintf("Fetched %s: %d
bytes", url, len(body))
}
```

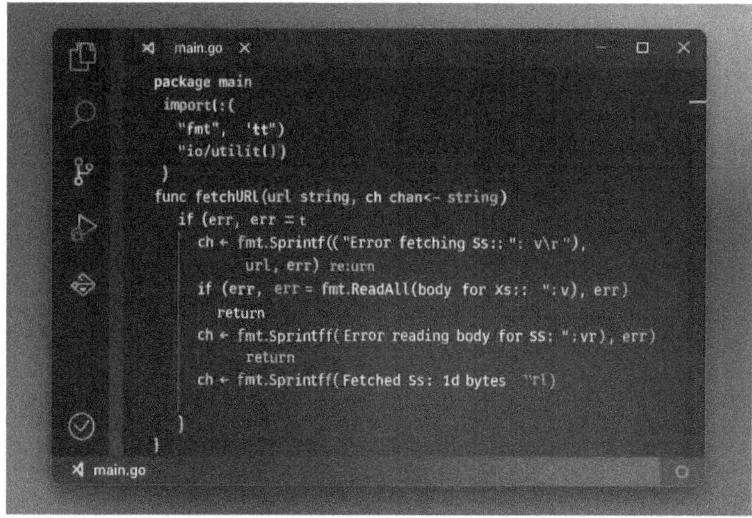

In the function fetchURL, we:

- Use http.Get to make a GET request to the specified URL.

- Read the response body and send a message to the channel with the result.

Step 2: Use Goroutines and Channels to Fetch Multiple URLs

Now, we'll use goroutines to fetch multiple URLs concurrently.

```go
func main() {
    urls := []string{
        "https://www.example.com",
        "https://www.golang.org",
        "https://www.github.com",
    }

    ch := make(chan string) // Create a
channel to receive results

    // Launch goroutines for each URL
    for _, url := range urls {
        go fetchURL(url, ch)
    }
```

```
    // Wait for all goroutines to
finish
    for range urls {
        fmt.Println(<-ch)
    }
}
```

In the main function:

- We define a list of URLs to scrape.
- We start a goroutine for each URL.
- We then print the results as they come in from the channel.

Step 3: Handling Errors Gracefully

The example includes error handling for both the HTTP request and the response body reading. If there's any error, the goroutine sends an error message to the channel.

Advanced Techniques & Optimization

Optimizing Concurrency with Goroutines

When you are dealing with a large number of goroutines, it's important to manage resources efficiently. Here are some best practices for optimizing goroutines and channels:

- **Limit Goroutines**: Too many goroutines can overwhelm the system. Use **worker pools** to limit the number of concurrent tasks.
- **Buffering Channels**: Buffered channels can help manage concurrency by allowing goroutines to send data to the channel without blocking.

Scalability Considerations

As you scale your application, consider using a combination of goroutines and channels to process data in parallel, but be mindful of memory usage and system limitations. Use profiling tools like pprof to identify bottlenecks.

Troubleshooting and Problem-Solving

Common Issues

- **Deadlocks**: Deadlocks occur when two or more goroutines are waiting on each other to complete, leading to a program freeze. This can often be avoided by carefully designing the synchronization logic.
- **Unbuffered Channels**: If you're using unbuffered channels, be aware that sending

and receiving data requires both sides to be ready. This can lead to blocking if not handled properly.

Conclusion & Next Steps

In this chapter, we've explored Go's concurrency model in detail, covering goroutines, channels, and the select statement. We've also built a practical web scraper to demonstrate these concepts in action. By understanding how to effectively manage concurrency in Go, you can build scalable, efficient applications that perform tasks concurrently with ease.

In the next chapter, we'll dive deeper into Go's standard library and explore how to work with file I/O, network programming, and other system-level operations. Keep experimenting with goroutines and channels to build more complex and powerful applications!

Chapter 5: Structs and Interfaces

Introduction

As you continue your Go programming journey, one key concept to master is how to work with **Structs** and **Interfaces**. While Go may not be a traditional object-oriented language, it offers powerful tools for managing complex data and implementing polymorphism. This chapter focuses on how to use **Structs** to define and group data, and **Interfaces** to define behavior and enable polymorphism in Go.

Why Structs and Interfaces Matter

In Go, **structs** provide a way to group different types of data into a single entity, while **interfaces** allow different types to implement shared behaviors. These concepts are fundamental to structuring programs in a way that is both readable and maintainable. Understanding how to use structs and interfaces will allow you to:

- **Model real-world objects**: Structs let you define complex objects with multiple fields, like a Product with fields for name, price, and quantity.
- **Leverage polymorphism**: Interfaces in Go allow different types to be treated as the same type if they implement the same methods, enabling you to write more flexible and reusable code.
- **Build scalable and maintainable applications**: The combination of structs and interfaces helps in creating modular code where each part can evolve independently.

In this chapter, we'll explore how to use these features in depth, with the goal of making you comfortable with defining and using structs and interfaces in Go. By the end, you will also have worked through a hands-on project: a **simple inventory management system** that uses structs and interfaces to perform CRUD (Create, Read, Update, Delete) operations on different types of products.

What You'll Learn in This Chapter:

- **Working with Structs**: How to define, instantiate, and use structs to group data.
- **Struct Composition and Embedding**: How to extend structs through composition and embedding.
- **Understanding Interfaces**: How to define interfaces, implement them, and achieve polymorphism.

- **Hands-on Project:** Build a simple inventory management system that uses structs and interfaces to manage different product types.

Core Concepts and Theory

1. Working with Structs

Structs are the primary way to define custom data types in Go. A **struct** is a composite data type that groups together variables (fields) under a single name. Structs allow you to model real-world entities such as products, orders, or users.

Defining Structs

To define a struct in Go, you use the type keyword, followed by the struct name and the struct keyword.

go

```
type Product struct {
    Name     string
    Price    float64
    Quantity int
}
```

In this example, we define a Product struct with three fields: Name, Price, and Quantity.

Instantiating Structs

You can create an instance of a struct in the following ways:

```go
// Using field names
product1 := Product{Name: "Laptop",
Price: 999.99, Quantity: 10}

// Without field names (note the order
must match the struct definition)
product2 := Product{"Phone", 499.99,
50}
```

The first method uses **named fields**, while the second uses **positional fields**, which can be error-prone if the struct definition changes later.

Accessing Struct Fields

Once you have a struct instance, you can access its fields using the dot (.) operator.

```go
fmt.Println(product1.Name)  // Output: Laptop
fmt.Println(product1.Price) // Output: 999.99
```

Pointer to Structs

In Go, structs are passed by value, meaning when you pass a struct to a function, it gets copied. If you need to modify the original struct, you must pass a pointer to the struct.

```go
go

func updateQuantity(p *Product,
quantity int) {
    p.Quantity = quantity
}

func main() {
    p := Product{Name: "Tablet", Price:
249.99, Quantity: 20}
    updateQuantity(&p, 30)
    fmt.Println(p.Quantity)  // Output:
30
}
```

Passing a pointer to updateQuantity allows it to modify the original Product struct.

---

2. Struct Composition and Embedding

Go doesn't support traditional inheritance, but it allows **composition** and **embedding** of structs.

This means you can create more complex structs by embedding simpler ones.

Composition

Composition refers to including one struct within another, allowing you to combine their fields and methods. For instance, you can have a Category struct that includes a Product struct.

```go
go

type Category struct {
    Name    string
    Product Product
}

category := Category{Name:
"Electronics", Product:
Product{"Laptop", 999.99, 10}}
fmt.Println(category.Product.Name) //
Output: Laptop
```

Struct Embedding

Go also allows **struct embedding**, where a struct can directly include another struct, and you can access the embedded struct's fields and methods without explicitly referencing them.

```go
type Item struct {
    Product
    SKU string
}

item := Item{Product:
Product{"Monitor", 150.00, 15}, SKU:
"A123"}
fmt.Println(item.Name) // Output:
Monitor
fmt.Println(item.SKU)  // Output: A123
```

In the above example, the Item struct embeds the Product struct, and you can directly access the Name field of Product from Item.

3. Understanding Interfaces

Interfaces in Go allow you to define behaviors (methods) that types must implement. Interfaces enable **polymorphism**, which means that a variable of an interface type can hold any type that implements the interface methods.

Defining an Interface

To define an interface, you simply list the methods that any type must implement.

```go
type Describable interface {
    Describe() string
}
```

This Describable interface requires a Describe method, but doesn't specify what the method does or how it's implemented.

Implementing Interfaces

Go doesn't require you to explicitly declare that a type implements an interface. As long as a type provides the required methods, it implements the interface automatically.

```go
type Product struct {
    Name     string
    Price    float64
    Quantity int
}

func (p Product) Describe() string {
    return fmt.Sprintf("Product: %s,
Price: %.2f", p.Name, p.Price)
}

func printDescription(d Describable) {
    fmt.Println(d.Describe())
}
```

```
func main() {
    p := Product{"Laptop", 999.99, 10}
    printDescription(p)  // Output:
Product: Laptop, Price: 999.99
}
```

Here, Product implements the Describable interface by defining a Describe method. The function printDescription accepts any type that implements the Describable interface.

Empty Interface

The empty interface interface{} is a special interface in Go. It doesn't require any methods, so any type can satisfy the empty interface. It's used when you want to handle any type dynamically.

```
go

var x interface{}
x = 42
fmt.Println(x) // Output: 42
x = "Hello"
```

```
fmt.Println(x) // Output: Hello
```

4. Polymorphism with Interfaces

Interfaces enable polymorphism in Go. By allowing different types to implement the same interface, Go enables you to write more flexible and reusable code. You can use an interface to interact with different types that share common behavior.

Example of Polymorphism

Let's extend the Describable interface to have different implementations for different types of products.

```go
go

type Describable interface {
    Describe() string
}

type Product struct {
    Name  string
```

```
    Price float64
}

func (p Product) Describe() string {
    return fmt.Sprintf("Product: %s,
Price: %.2f", p.Name, p.Price)
}

type Service struct {
    Name string
    Fee  float64
}

func (s Service) Describe() string {
    return fmt.Sprintf("Service: %s,
Fee: %.2f", s.Name, s.Fee)
}

func printDescription(d Describable) {
    fmt.Println(d.Describe())
}

func main() {
    p := Product{"Laptop", 999.99}
    s := Service{"Consulting", 150.00}
```

```
    printDescription(p) // Output:
Product: Laptop, Price: 999.99
    printDescription(s) // Output:
Service: Consulting, Fee: 150.00
}
```

Here, both Product and Service implement the Describe method, making them both compatible with the Describable interface. The printDescription function works with both types, showcasing polymorphism in Go.

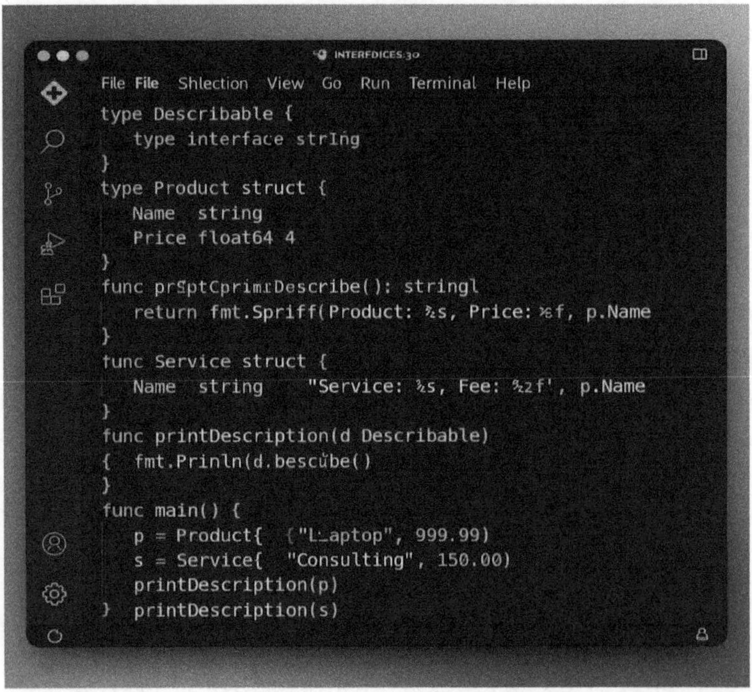

Tools and Setup

Before we dive into the hands-on project, ensure you have the following tools set up:

- **Go Programming Language**: Make sure you have Go installed on your machine. If you haven't done so yet, refer to Chapter 1 for installation instructions.
- **Text Editor or IDE**: A code editor or Integrated Development Environment (IDE) that supports Go is essential. Some great options include:
    - **Visual Studio Code** with the Go extension for Go support.
    - **GoLand** by JetBrains, a full-featured Go IDE.
- **Version Control (Optional)**: If you're working on multiple projects, consider

using Git for version control to manage changes to your code.

Hands-On Examples & Projects

Building a Simple Inventory Management System

In this project, we'll create a simple **Inventory Management System** using structs and interfaces. The system will allow us to manage different product types, with functionality for CRUD (Create, Read, Update, Delete) operations.

Step 1: Define Structs for Products

We will start by defining the basic struct to represent a product:

```go
package main

import "fmt"
```

```
type Product struct {
    ID       int
    Name     string
    Category string
    Price    float64
    Quantity int
}

func (p *Product) UpdateQuantity(qty
int) {
    p.Quantity = qty
}
```

In this example, we define the Product struct with fields like ID, Name, Category, Price, and Quantity. We also define a method UpdateQuantity that will allow us to update the quantity of a product.

Step 2: Create the Interface for CRUD Operations

Next, we define an interface for managing products:

```go
go

type Inventory interface {
    AddProduct(product Product)
    GetProduct(id int) (Product, error)
    UpdateProduct(id int, product
Product) error
    DeleteProduct(id int) error
}
```

This interface defines the methods needed for CRUD operations: adding, retrieving, updating, and deleting products.

Step 3: Implement the Interface

Now we'll create a struct that will implement the Inventory interface:

```go
go

type InventoryManager struct {
    products map[int]Product
}
```

```
func (im *InventoryManager)
AddProduct(p Product) {
    im.products[p.ID] = p
}

func (im *InventoryManager)
GetProduct(id int) (Product, error) {
    if product, exists :=
im.products[id]; exists {
        return product, nil
    }
    return Product{},
fmt.Errorf("product not found")
}

func (im *InventoryManager)
UpdateProduct(id int, p Product) error
{
    if _, exists := im.products[id];
exists {
        im.products[id] = p
        return nil
    }
    return fmt.Errorf("product not
found")
```

```
}

func (im *InventoryManager)
DeleteProduct(id int) error {
    if _, exists := im.products[id];
exists {
        delete(im.products, id)
        return nil
    }
    return fmt.Errorf("product not
found")
}
```

Here, the InventoryManager struct implements all the methods defined in the Inventory interface. It uses a map to store products.

Step 4: Implement CRUD Operations in Main

Finally, we'll implement a simple main function that uses these methods:

```
go

func main() {
```

```
    im := &InventoryManager{products:
make(map[int]Product)}

    product1 := Product{ID: 1, Name:
"Laptop", Category: "Electronics",
Price: 999.99, Quantity: 10}
    im.AddProduct(product1)

    product2 := Product{ID: 2, Name:
"Phone", Category: "Electronics",
Price: 599.99, Quantity: 50}
    im.AddProduct(product2)

    // Get product by ID
    p, err := im.GetProduct(1)
    if err != nil {
        fmt.Println(err)
    } else {
        fmt.Println(p)
    }

    // Update product quantity
    im.UpdateProduct(1, Product{ID: 1,
Name: "Laptop", Category:
```

```
"Electronics", Price: 999.99, Quantity:
20})

    // Delete a product
    im.DeleteProduct(2)

    fmt.Println(im.products)
}
```

Here, we initialize the inventory manager, add products, retrieve a product by ID, update a product, and delete a product. This is a full-fledged CRUD operation.

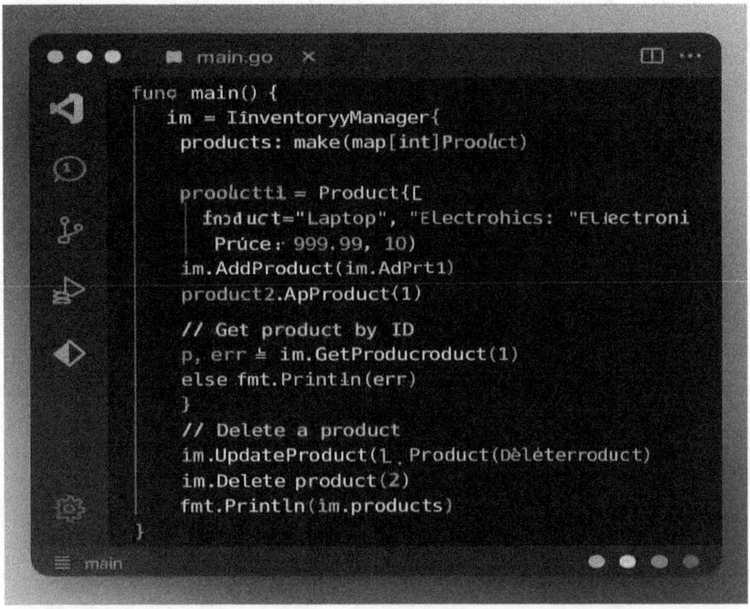

Advanced Techniques & Optimization

Optimizing CRUD Operations

- **Concurrency**: If your inventory system needs to support multiple users, consider using goroutines and channels to handle concurrent updates or queries.
- **Database Integration**: For a more complex inventory system, you may want to integrate a database such as MySQL or PostgreSQL to persist data.

Performance Considerations

- **Data Size**: If you anticipate dealing with large amounts of data, you may want to explore memory management strategies like caching frequently accessed products.

- **Database vs. In-Memory:** For large-scale systems, an in-memory map like we used may not suffice. Consider using a database for persistence.

Troubleshooting and Problem-Solving

Common Challenges

- **Nil Pointer Dereferencing:** When using structs, ensure that pointers are properly initialized. For example, passing a nil pointer to a method will cause a runtime panic.
- **Handling Errors:** Always handle errors gracefully, especially in CRUD operations where the product might not exist.

Conclusion & Next Steps

By now, you've learned how to work with structs and interfaces in Go, and you've built a simple inventory management system. You've also explored how Go handles polymorphism through interfaces, allowing for more flexible and reusable code. This foundational knowledge will help you as you build more complex systems.

In the next chapter, we'll dive into Go's error handling mechanisms, exploring how to create robust and reliable applications that can gracefully handle failure. Keep experimenting with structs and interfaces, and continue refining your understanding of Go's powerful features!

Chapter 6: Advanced Go Features for Professionals

Introduction

As you progress in your Go programming journey, you will inevitably encounter situations that require deeper insights and advanced features. While Go's simplicity and minimalism are what make it so appealing, it's also a powerful language capable of tackling complex programming challenges. This chapter explores some of Go's most advanced features, such as **reflection**, **testing**, and **advanced concurrency patterns**, which are essential for building robust, scalable, and high-performance applications.

Why You Should Care

In a professional environment, mastering advanced features of Go will allow you to handle more complex tasks and optimize your applications for real-world use. Whether you're dealing with dynamic data structures, writing unit tests to ensure correctness, or handling concurrent processes efficiently, these advanced concepts will elevate your development skills.

What You Will Learn:

- **Reflection in Go**: How to inspect and manipulate Go types at runtime using the reflect package.
- **Testing in Go**: Learn about unit testing and test-driven development (TDD) to ensure your code is reliable and robust.
- **Concurrency Deep Dive**: Explore advanced patterns for concurrent programming using goroutines and channels.

- **Hands-On Project:** Build a **stock market simulation** that uses advanced concurrency features to simulate buy and sell transactions in parallel.

This chapter is designed for developers who are already familiar with basic Go programming and want to take their skills to the next level. By the end of this chapter, you'll not only have a solid grasp of advanced Go features but also the ability to write more maintainable, scalable, and high-performance Go applications.

Core Concepts and Theory

1. Reflection: What Is It and How to Use It

In Go, **reflection** allows you to inspect and manipulate types at runtime. This feature is particularly useful when you need to interact with types whose structure is not known at compile time. While reflection can be a powerful tool, it should be used judiciously as it can reduce performance and lead to more complex code.

Using the reflect Package

Go’s reflect package provides functionality to inspect the type and value of objects at runtime. Here's a breakdown of key functions in reflect:

- **reflect.TypeOf()**: Returns the type of a value.
- **reflect.ValueOf()**: Returns the value of a variable.
- **reflect.Kind**: Represents the kind of type, such as int, string, struct, etc.

Example of reflection in Go:

```go
go

package main
```

```
import (
    "fmt"
    "reflect"
)

type Product struct {
    Name  string
    Price float64
}

func main() {
    p := Product{Name: "Laptop", Price:
999.99}

    t := reflect.TypeOf(p)       // Get
the type of 'p'
    v := reflect.ValueOf(p)      // Get
the value of 'p'

    fmt.Println("Type:", t)       //
Output: Type: main.Product
    fmt.Println("Value:", v)      //
Output: {Laptop 999.99}
    fmt.Println("Field 1:", v.Field(0))
// Output: Laptop
```

```
    fmt.Println("Field 2:", v.Field(1))
// Output: 999.99
}
```

In this example:

- reflect.TypeOf(p) returns the type of Product.
- reflect.ValueOf(p) returns the value of the struct p.
- The Field method allows access to the individual fields of a struct.

Modifying Struct Fields with Reflection

One powerful aspect of reflection is the ability to modify fields in a struct at runtime. This can be done by first obtaining a pointer to the struct and then using Set on the reflect value.

```
go

func setPrice(p *Product, newPrice
float64) {
```

```
    v := reflect.ValueOf(p).Elem() //
Get the value of the pointer
    priceField :=
v.FieldByName("Price")
    if priceField.IsValid() &&
priceField.CanSet() {
        priceField.SetFloat(newPrice)
    }
}

func main() {
    p := &Product{Name: "Laptop",
Price: 999.99}
    setPrice(p, 1199.99)
    fmt.Println("Updated Product
Price:", p.Price)  // Output: 1199.99
}
```

In this example:

- Elem() is used to dereference the pointer to the struct.
- SetFloat() is used to change the value of the Price field.

Reflection Limitations

- **Performance**: Reflection is slower than direct manipulation of types, and should be avoided in performance-critical code.
- **Type Safety**: Using reflection reduces type safety, as it bypasses Go's strong typing system.

---

2. Testing: Unit Testing and Test-Driven Development (TDD)

Testing is crucial for maintaining code quality and ensuring that your application works as expected. Go includes a built-in testing framework in the testing package, which is straightforward to use for writing unit tests.

Unit Testing in Go

A unit test in Go is a function that tests a specific part of your code, usually a function. Unit tests are placed in files ending with _test.go.

Example of a unit test:

```go
go

package main

import "testing"

// Function to add two numbers
func add(a, b int) int {
    return a + b
}

// Unit test for the add function
func TestAdd(t *testing.T) {
    result := add(2, 3)
    if result != 5 {
        t.Errorf("Expected 5, got %d",
result)
```

```
    }
}
```

To run the test:

```shell

$ go test
```

In this example:

- We define the add function and a test function TestAdd.
- t.Errorf is used to report a failure if the result is not what we expect.

Test-Driven Development (TDD)

Test-Driven Development (TDD) is a software development process in which you write tests before writing the actual code. TDD follows a simple cycle:

1. **Red**: Write a failing test.

2. **Green**: Write the minimal code needed to pass the test.
3. **Refactor**: Refactor the code while keeping the tests passing.

Using TDD helps you design better code by focusing on the desired behavior first. In Go, the simplicity of the testing framework makes TDD an effective approach.

---

3. Go Routines and Channels: Advanced Patterns

Go's concurrency model is one of its standout features. In this section, we'll explore advanced concurrency patterns using **goroutines** and **channels**, which allow you to efficiently handle parallel tasks in your applications.

Worker Pools

A **worker pool** is a common concurrency pattern in which a fixed number of goroutines are used to process tasks concurrently. This pattern is useful when you need to limit the number of concurrent operations but still achieve parallelism.

Here's an example of a worker pool:

```go
package main

import "fmt"

type Job struct {
    id    int
    value int
}

type Worker struct {
    id         int
```

```
    jobChannel chan Job
}

func (w *Worker) start() {
    for job := range w.jobChannel {
        fmt.Printf("Worker %d
processing job %d with value %d\n",
w.id, job.id, job.value)
    }
}

func main() {
    jobChannel := make(chan Job)
    workers := []Worker{
        {id: 1, jobChannel:
jobChannel},
        {id: 2, jobChannel:
jobChannel},
    }

    for i := range workers {
        go workers[i].start()
    }

    for i := 1; i <= 5; i++ {
```

```
        jobChannel <- Job{id: i, value: i * 10}
    }

    close(jobChannel)
}
```

In this example:

- We create two workers that each process jobs concurrently.
- The main function sends jobs to the jobChannel that workers are reading from.

Buffered Channels and Select Patterns

Buffered channels allow goroutines to send data to a channel without blocking, as long as there is space in the buffer. This is useful for managing load and reducing the number of blocking operations in your program.

The select statement can be used to wait on multiple channels concurrently. It's a powerful way to handle multiple sources of data without blocking.

```go
go

ch1 := make(chan string, 2)
ch2 := make(chan string, 2)

select {
case msg1 := <-ch1:
    fmt.Println("Received from ch1:",
msg1)
case msg2 := <-ch2:
    fmt.Println("Received from ch2:",
msg2)
}
```

In this example:

- The select statement waits on multiple channels and processes whichever channel is ready first.

Tools and Setup

To complete this chapter, you will need:

- **Go** installed on your system. If you haven't already done so, please refer to Chapter 1 for installation instructions.
- **Text Editor or IDE**: While any text editor will do, using an IDE like **Visual Studio Code** (with Go extensions) or **GoLand** will significantly improve your productivity.
- **Testing Framework**: Go's built-in testing package is everything you need for writing unit tests.
- **Concurrency Setup**: No additional setup is required for concurrency as Go's goroutines and channels are part of the standard library.

Ensure your environment is configured as described, and you are ready to start experimenting with advanced Go features.

Hands-On Examples & Projects

Building a Stock Market Simulation

In this section, we'll build a simple **stock market simulation.** The simulation will allow users to perform buy and sell transactions concurrently, using advanced concurrency features like goroutines and channels.

Step 1: Define the Stock and Transaction Structs

We will define a Stock struct to represent a stock's price and quantity, and a Transaction struct to represent buy and sell transactions.

go

```
type Stock struct {
    Symbol  string
    Price   float64
    Quantity int
}

type Transaction struct {
    Stock   Stock
    Amount  int
    Action  string // "buy" or "sell"
}
```

Step 2: Create Functions for Transactions

We will create functions to handle the buy and sell transactions. Each transaction will modify the stock's quantity and price.

```
go

func buy(stock *Stock, amount int) {
    stock.Quantity += amount
```

```
    stock.Price *= 1.02 // Assume a 2%
price increase on buy
}

func sell(stock *Stock, amount int) {
    if stock.Quantity >= amount {
        stock.Quantity -= amount
        stock.Price *= 0.98 // Assume a
2% price decrease on sell
    } else {
        fmt.Println("Not enough stock
to sell!")
    }
}
```

Step 3: Use Goroutines for Concurrent Transactions

We will simulate multiple users performing transactions concurrently using goroutines.

```
go
```

```
func handleTransaction(ch chan<-
string, transaction Transaction, stock
*Stock) {
    if transaction.Action == "buy" {
        buy(stock, transaction.Amount)
    } else if transaction.Action ==
"sell" {
        sell(stock, transaction.Amount)
    }
    ch <- fmt.Sprintf("Transaction
complete: %s %d %s stock",
transaction.Action, transaction.Amount,
stock.Symbol)
}

func main() {
    stock := &Stock{Symbol: "AAPL",
Price: 150.00, Quantity: 100}

    ch := make(chan string)

    transactions := []Transaction{
        {Stock: *stock, Amount: 10,
Action: "buy"},
```

```
        {Stock: *stock, Amount: 5,
Action: "sell"},
        {Stock: *stock, Amount: 15,
Action: "buy"},
    }

    for _, transaction := range
transactions {
        go handleTransaction(ch,
transaction, stock)
    }

    for range transactions {
        fmt.Println(<-ch)
    }

    fmt.Printf("Final stock status:
%v\n", stock)
}
```

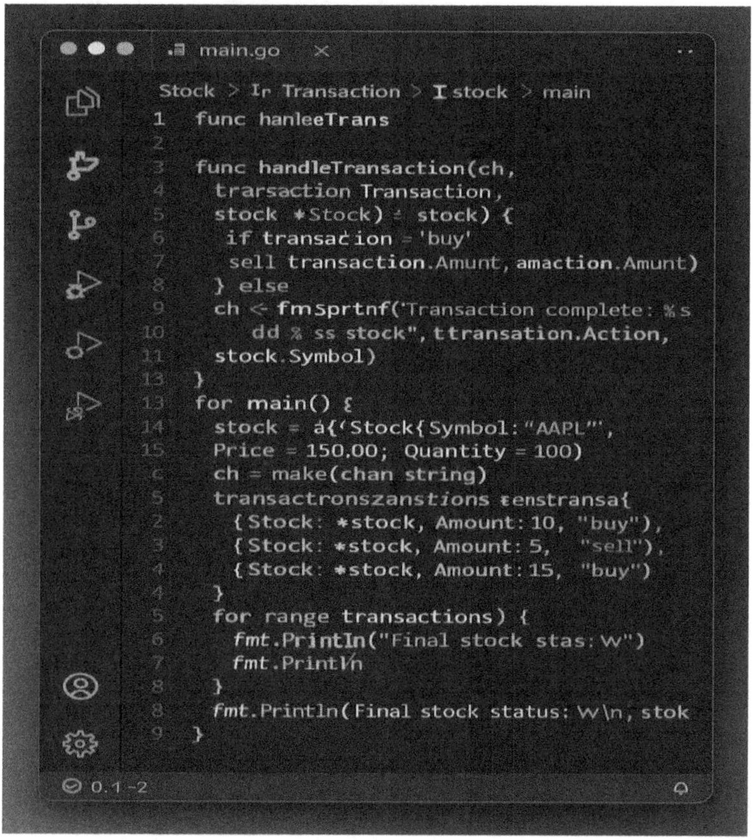

```
main.go
Stock > Ir Transaction > I stock > main
func hanleeTrans

func handleTransaction(ch,
  trarsaction Transaction,
  stock *Stock) = stock) {
   if transaction = 'buy'
   sell transaction.Amunt, amaction.Amunt)
  } else
  ch <- fmSprtnf('Transaction complete: %s
     dd % ss stock", ttransation.Action,
  stock.Symbol)
}
for main() {
  stock = a{'Stock{Symbol:"AAPL"',
  Price = 150.00; Quantity = 100)
  ch = make(chan string)
  transactronszanstions tenstransa{
    {Stock: *stock, Amount: 10, "buy"),
    {Stock: *stock, Amount: 5,  "sell"),
    {Stock: *stock, Amount: 15, "buy")
  }
  for range transactions) {
    fmt.Println("Final stock stas: W")
    fmt.PrintVn
  }
  fmt.Println(Final stock status: W\n, stok
}
0.1 -2
```

Step 4: Running the Simulation

- This code simulates multiple transactions on the same stock concurrently.
- Goroutines handle each transaction (buy or sell).

- The main function waits for all transactions to complete and then prints the final stock status.

Advanced Techniques & Optimization

Optimizing Concurrency

- **Worker Pools**: If you need to manage many concurrent tasks, consider using a worker pool pattern to limit the number of goroutines.
- **Buffering Channels**: Use buffered channels for controlling load and minimizing blocking operations.

Performance Considerations

- **Minimize Memory Usage**: Efficient memory management can be crucial for large-scale simulations or applications. Always be mindful of the number of goroutines you spawn.

Troubleshooting and Problem-Solving

Common Issues

- **Deadlocks**: When channels are unbuffered, it's easy to run into deadlocks where goroutines are waiting for each other. Use buffered channels or the select statement to avoid blocking.
- **Race Conditions**: When multiple goroutines access shared data, you can run into race conditions. Ensure data is properly synchronized using channels or sync.Mutex.

Conclusion & Next Steps

Congratulations on completing this advanced chapter on Go! You've learned about reflection, testing, and advanced concurrency patterns, and you've built a stock market simulation that takes full advantage of Go's powerful concurrency model.

To continue your learning journey, consider exploring more advanced Go topics, such as building web services with Go, working with databases, or implementing microservices architectures. Keep experimenting with goroutines and channels to solve real-world problems, and apply the principles of test-driven development to ensure that your code remains reliable and maintainable.

Chapter 7: Go in the Real World

Introduction

In the world of modern software development, the ability to write code that is efficient, scalable, and easy to maintain is critical. Go (Golang) has proven to be one of the best languages for building high-performance systems, especially for networked applications, databases, and APIs. This chapter explores Go's real-world applications by diving into the specifics of building web servers, interfacing with databases, and developing APIs. By focusing on these topics, we will show you how to leverage Go's simplicity and power to create practical, scalable solutions.

Why You Should Care

As a professional Go developer, you will often need to design and implement web services, handle persistent storage in databases, and build systems that can scale to handle a high volume of requests. These are the kinds of tasks that Go excels at, thanks to its concurrency model, simplicity, and speed.

Throughout this chapter, you will explore real-world scenarios that Go developers often encounter. You'll start by creating a basic HTTP server using Go's built-in net/http package and progress to building a complete RESTful API. Additionally, you'll see how to interface with SQL databases (like PostgreSQL or MySQL) and perform CRUD (Create, Read, Update, Delete) operations.

Finally, we'll culminate with a hands-on project: a **simple blog application** where users can create, read, update, and delete blog posts through an API. This project will give you practical experience with the concepts covered in the chapter, reinforcing your understanding and helping you apply these skills in the real world.

What You Will Learn:

- **Building Web Servers**: Learn how to create a basic HTTP server with Go, handle routing, and serve dynamic content.
- **Interfacing with Databases**: Understand how to connect Go to SQL databases like PostgreSQL and MySQL and perform CRUD operations.
- **Developing APIs**: Build RESTful APIs with Go, using the net/http package and third-party libraries such as gorilla/mux.

- **Hands-on Project:** Build a simple blog application that allows users to create, read, update, and delete posts via an API.

By the end of this chapter, you will have the skills to apply Go in real-world scenarios, from web server development to creating APIs and managing databases.

Core Concepts and Theory

1. Building Web Servers in Go

Go provides an easy-to-use package, net/http, which is perfect for building web servers. It allows you to create HTTP servers that can handle different HTTP methods like GET, POST, PUT, and DELETE.

Creating a Basic HTTP Server

To create a basic HTTP server, you need to use the http.ListenAndServe() function, which listens on a port and handles incoming HTTP requests.

Example:

```
go

package main

import (
    "fmt"
    "log"
    "net/http"
)

// handler function to handle requests
to the root URL
func handler(w http.ResponseWriter, r
*http.Request) {
    fmt.Fprintf(w, "Hello, Go Web
Server!")
}

func main() {
    // Register the handler function
with the default mux
    http.HandleFunc("/", handler)
```

```
// Start the server on port 8080

log.Fatal(http.ListenAndServe(":8080",
nil))
}
```

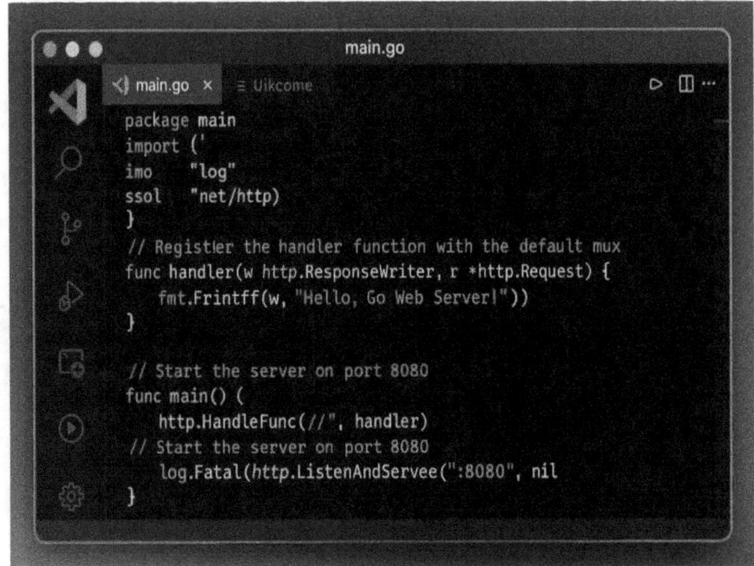

- **http.HandleFunc("/", handler)**: This function maps the / URL path to the handler function. When users visit the root of the server, the handler will be executed.
- **http.ListenAndServe(":8080", nil)**: This starts the web server on port 8080 and listens for incoming requests.

Routing and Serving Dynamic Content

Go's net/http package includes basic routing functionality, but you can also use third-party packages, such as **gorilla/mux**, for more advanced routing capabilities. mux supports variables in paths, more flexible route handling, and more.

Example with gorilla/mux:

```
go

package main

import (
	"fmt"
	"github.com/gorilla/mux"
	"log"
	"net/http"
)

func main() {
	r := mux.NewRouter()

	// Define routes and handlers
```

```
    r.HandleFunc("/", func(w
http.ResponseWriter, r *http.Request) {
        fmt.Fprintf(w, "Welcome to the
homepage!")
    })

    r.HandleFunc("/post/{id:[0-9]+}",
func(w http.ResponseWriter, r
*http.Request) {
        vars := mux.Vars(r)
        postID := vars["id"]
        fmt.Fprintf(w, "Viewing post
with ID: %s", postID)
    })


log.Fatal(http.ListenAndServe(":8080",
r))
}
```

In this example:

- We use gorilla/mux to define a route that accepts a dynamic id parameter (/post/{id:[0-9]+}).

- This enables us to build a RESTful structure where paths and parameters are part of the URL.

2. Interfacing with Databases

Connecting Go to databases is a crucial skill for developers working with real-world applications. Go supports several database management systems (DBMS), including SQL databases like PostgreSQL, MySQL, and SQLite.

Connecting to PostgreSQL or MySQL

Go's database/sql package provides a database-agnostic interface to interact with relational databases. You can use Go's database/sql package along with a driver (e.g., pq for PostgreSQL or mysql for MySQL).

Connecting to PostgreSQL

Here's how to connect to a PostgreSQL database using the pq driver:

```go
go

package main

import (
    "database/sql"
    "fmt"
    "log"
    _ "github.com/lib/pq"
)

const (
    host     = "localhost"
    port     = 5432
    user     = "your_user"
    password = "your_password"
    dbname   = "your_dbname"
)

func main() {
    // Build the connection string
    psqlInfo := fmt.Sprintf("host=%s
port=%d user=%s password=%s dbname=%s
sslmode=disable",
```

```
        host, port, user, password,
dbname)

    // Open a connection to the
database
    db, err := sql.Open("postgres",
psqlInfo)
    if err != nil {
        log.Fatal(err)
    }

    // Ping the database to check if
the connection is working
    err = db.Ping()
    if err != nil {
        log.Fatal(err)
    }

    fmt.Println("Successfully connected
to the database!")
}
```

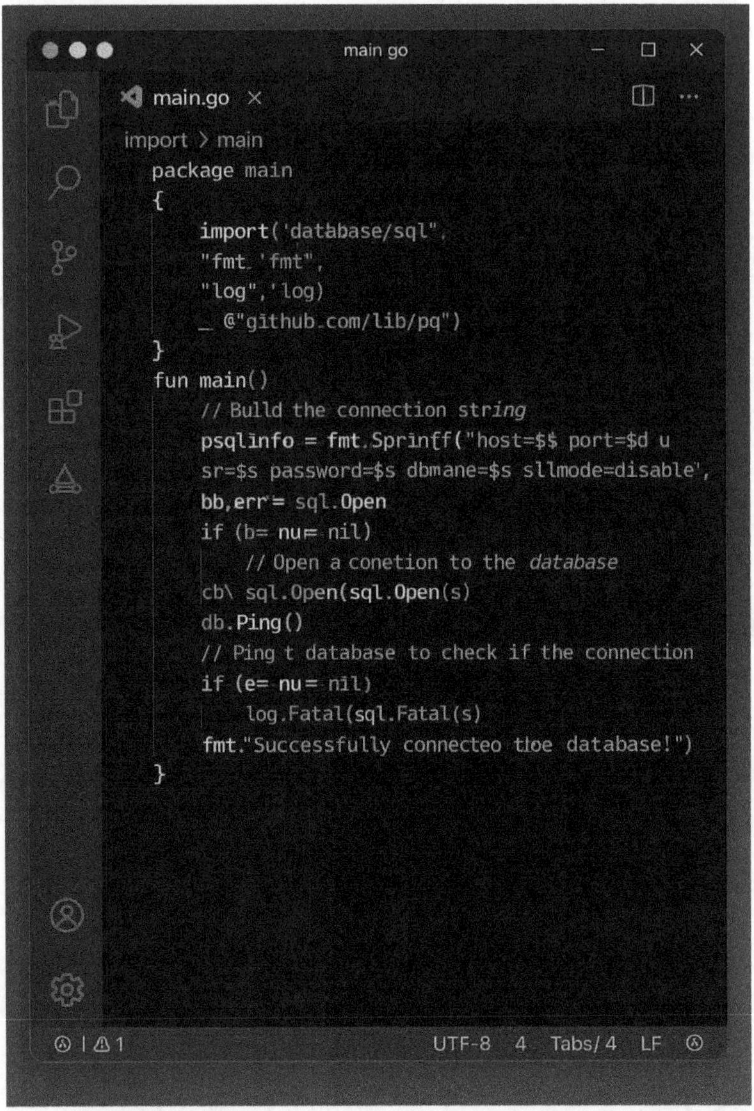

```
main go
main.go
import > main
package main
{
    import('database/sql",
    "fmt. 'fmt",
    "log",'log)
    _ @"github.com/lib/pq")
}
fun main()
    // Bulld the connection string
    psqlinfo = fmt.Sprinff("host=$$ port=$d u
    sr=$s password=$s dbmane=$s sllmode=disable',
    bb,err= sql.Open
    if (b= nu= nil)
        // Open a conetion to the database
    cb\ sql.Open(sql.Open(s)
    db.Ping()
    // Ping t database to check if the connection
    if (e= nu= nil)
        log.Fatal(sql.Fatal(s)
    fmt."Successfully connecteo tloe database!")
}
UTF-8  4  Tabs/4  LF
```

- **sql.Open()**: Opens a database connection with the provided connection string.

- **db.Ping()**: Verifies that the connection is active.

Performing CRUD Operations

Once connected, you can perform CRUD operations (Create, Read, Update, Delete) on the database. Here's an example of performing a simple INSERT and SELECT operation.

```go
// Create a new product
func createProduct(db *sql.DB, name
string, price float64) {
    query := `INSERT INTO products
(name, price) VALUES ($1, $2)`
    _, err := db.Exec(query, name,
price)
    if err != nil {
        log.Fatal(err)
    }
    fmt.Println("Product created
successfully!")
}
```

```
// Read products from the database
func getProducts(db *sql.DB) {
    rows, err := db.Query("SELECT id,
name, price FROM products")
    if err != nil {
        log.Fatal(err)
    }
    defer rows.Close()

    for rows.Next() {
        var id int
        var name string
        var price float64
        if err := rows.Scan(&id, &name,
&price); err != nil {
            log.Fatal(err)
        }
        fmt.Printf("Product ID: %d,
Name: %s, Price: %.2f\n", id, name,
price)
    }
}
```

- db.Exec(): Executes a query that modifies the database (e.g., INSERT, UPDATE, DELETE).
- db.Query(): Executes a query that retrieves data from the database.

---

3. Developing APIs in Go

Developing APIs is one of the most common use cases for Go, especially when building microservices or integrating with front-end applications. Go's net/http package provides the necessary tools to build a simple RESTful API. However, for more advanced routing and features, the gorilla/mux library is a great choice.

Building a RESTful API

A RESTful API allows users to perform CRUD operations over HTTP. The most common

HTTP methods used in REST are GET, POST, PUT, and DELETE.

Here's an example of building a simple RESTful API in Go that allows users to perform CRUD operations on blog posts:

```
go

package main

import (
    "encoding/json"
    "fmt"
    "net/http"
    "github.com/gorilla/mux"
)

type Post struct {
    ID      string `json:"id"`
    Title   string `json:"title"`
    Content string `json:"content"`
}
```

```
var posts []Post

func createPost(w http.ResponseWriter,
r *http.Request) {
    var post Post
    err :=
json.NewDecoder(r.Body).Decode(&post)
    if err != nil {
        http.Error(w, err.Error(),
http.StatusBadRequest)
        return
    }

    posts = append(posts, post)
    w.WriteHeader(http.StatusCreated)
    json.NewEncoder(w).Encode(post)
}

func getPosts(w http.ResponseWriter, r
*http.Request) {
    w.Header().Set("Content-Type",
"application/json")
    json.NewEncoder(w).Encode(posts)
}
```

```
func getPost(w http.ResponseWriter, r
*http.Request) {
    params := mux.Vars(r)
    for _, post := range posts {
        if post.ID == params["id"] {
            w.Header().Set("Content-
Type", "application/json")

json.NewEncoder(w).Encode(post)
            return
        }
    }
    http.Error(w, "Post not found",
http.StatusNotFound)
}

func main() {
    router := mux.NewRouter()

    router.HandleFunc("/posts",
getPosts).Methods("GET")
    router.HandleFunc("/posts/{id}",
getPost).Methods("GET")
    router.HandleFunc("/posts",
createPost).Methods("POST")
```

```
    http.ListenAndServe(":8080",
router)
}
```

In this example:

- We define a Post struct to represent a blog post.
- We create three routes: one for getting all posts, one for getting a single post by ID, and one for creating a new post.
- The createPost function decodes the incoming JSON and adds the post to an in-memory list.
- The getPost function looks up a post by ID and returns it as a JSON response.

Tools and Setup

To complete this chapter, you'll need the following tools:

- **Go Programming Language**: Ensure you have Go installed on your machine. Refer to Chapter 1 for installation instructions.
- **SQL Database**: You can use PostgreSQL or MySQL for the database. If you don't have one installed, follow the respective documentation for installation.
- **Text Editor or IDE**: A good Go IDE like **GoLand** or **Visual Studio Code** (with Go extensions) will help you write, test, and debug your code more effectively.

Setting Up the Development Environment

1. **Install Go**: Download and install Go from the official website.
2. **Install Database**: Follow the installation guides for PostgreSQL or MySQL.
3. **Install gorilla/mux**: If you want to use the mux router, install it by running:

```swift
go get -u github.com/gorilla/mux
```

Hands-on Examples & Projects

Building a Blog Application with an API

In this section, we'll build a simple blog application where users can perform CRUD operations on posts via an API. This will require setting up an HTTP server, routing, handling database interactions, and serializing data in JSON format.

Step 1: Define the Post Model and API Routes

We've already defined the Post model and routes for handling the API. Let's extend the example by adding additional routes for updating and deleting posts.

```go
go

// Function to update a post
func updatePost(w http.ResponseWriter,
r *http.Request) {
    params := mux.Vars(r)
    var updatedPost Post
    err :=
json.NewDecoder(r.Body).Decode(&updated
Post)
    if err != nil {
        http.Error(w, err.Error(),
http.StatusBadRequest)
```

```
        return
    }

    for i, post := range posts {
        if post.ID == params["id"] {
            posts[i] = updatedPost
            w.Header().Set("Content-
Type", "application/json")

json.NewEncoder(w).Encode(updatedPost)
            return
        }
    }
    http.Error(w, "Post not found",
http.StatusNotFound)
}

// Function to delete a post
func deletePost(w http.ResponseWriter,
r *http.Request) {
    params := mux.Vars(r)
    for i, post := range posts {
        if post.ID == params["id"] {
            posts = append(posts[:i],
posts[i+1:]...)
```

```
w.WriteHeader(http.StatusNoContent)
            return
        }
    }
    http.Error(w, "Post not found",
http.StatusNotFound)
}
```

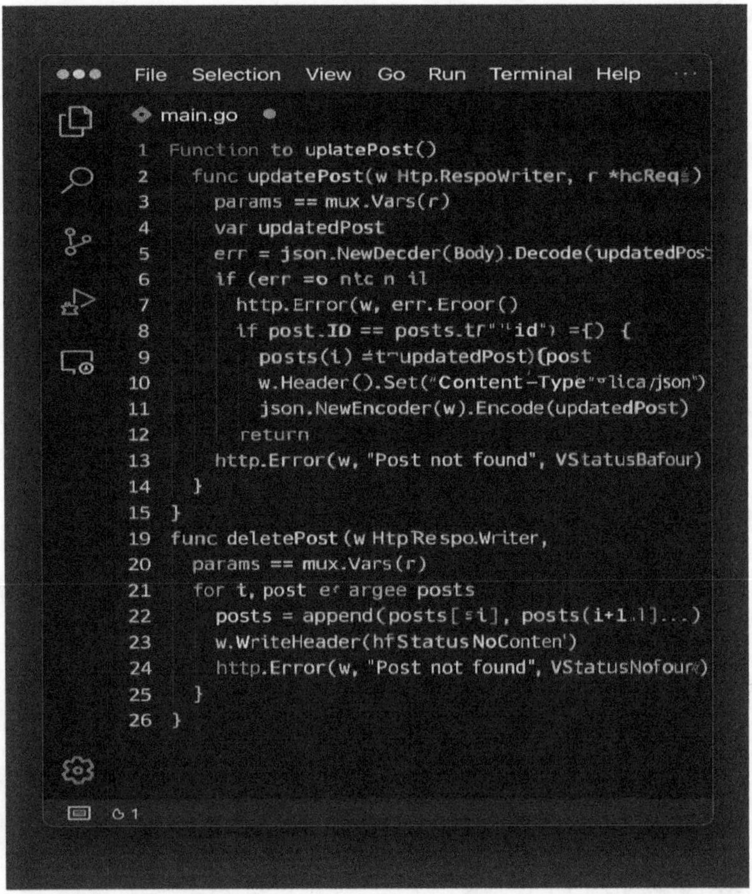

File Selection View Go Run Terminal Help

main.go

```
Function to uplatePost()
  func updatePost(w Htp.RespoWriter, r *hcReq)
    params == mux.Vars(r)
    var updatedPost
    err = json.NewDecder(Body).Decode(updatedPos
    if (err =o ntc n il
      http.Error(w, err.Eroor()
      if post.ID == posts.tr" "id") ={) {
        posts(i) =t updatedPost)(post
        w.Header().Set("Content-Type" lica/json")
        json.NewEncoder(w).Encode(updatedPost)
      return
    http.Error(w, "Post not found", VStatusBafour)
  }
}
func deletePost (w HtpRespo.Writer,
  params == mux.Vars(r)
  for i, post e argee posts
    posts = append(posts[ i], posts(i+1 1]...)
    w.WriteHeader(hfStatus NoConten')
    http.Error(w, "Post not found", VStatusNofour)
  }
}
```

Step 2: Run the Server and Test the API

After adding the updatePost and deletePost functions, run the server and use Postman or curl to test the API by making requests to the endpoints.

- **Create a Post**: Send a POST request to /posts with a JSON body.
- **Get All Posts**: Send a GET request to /posts.
- **Update a Post**: Send a PUT request to /posts/{id} with the updated post data.
- **Delete a Post**: Send a DELETE request to /posts/{id}.

Advanced Techniques & Optimization

Optimizing Concurrency in Go

When building APIs or web servers, concurrency is often a concern. Go's lightweight goroutines make it easy to handle many simultaneous requests. However, as the number of requests grows, you need to manage concurrency efficiently. Here are some strategies:

- **Worker Pools**: Limit the number of concurrent tasks with a worker pool to prevent overloading your system.
- **Database Connection Pooling**: Use a database connection pool to manage and reuse database connections, improving performance.

Scalability Considerations

- **Load Balancing:** In production systems, consider using a load balancer to distribute traffic across multiple instances of your application.
- **Caching:** For highly dynamic data, use caching to reduce the load on your database and speed up response times.

Troubleshooting and Problem-Solving

Common Issues

- **Database Connection Issues:** Ensure that your database credentials and configuration are correct. Use connection pooling for more efficient database management.

- **Concurrent Request Handling:** When handling multiple requests concurrently, be mindful of race conditions. Use Go's synchronization mechanisms, like sync.Mutex, when accessing shared resources.

Error Handling in Go

Go's error handling is simple but powerful. Always check for errors when performing actions like querying a database or making HTTP requests.

Conclusion & Next Steps

In this chapter, you have learned how to apply Go to real-world scenarios by building web servers, working with databases, and developing APIs. You've also had the chance to build a simple blog application that can handle CRUD operations via an API.

Next, you can continue learning about advanced Go features, such as working with concurrency in distributed systems, creating microservices with Go, and integrating Go with message queues like RabbitMQ or Kafka. Keep practicing by building more complex applications and expanding on the blog application you created in this chapter.

Chapter 8: Go and Cloud Computing

Introduction

Cloud computing has revolutionized the way we build and deploy applications, making it easier than ever to scale and manage systems. Go, with its simple syntax, powerful concurrency model, and ability to handle high-performance tasks, has become an ideal language for cloud-native applications. Whether you are deploying microservices, handling serverless computing, or building scalable backend systems, Go is well-suited for the cloud environment.

In this chapter, we will explore how to leverage Go's strengths to build and deploy scalable applications in the cloud. From building web servers to deploying containers, we will guide you through the process of getting your Go applications up and running on cloud platforms like AWS, Google Cloud, and Heroku. We will also take a deep dive into Docker and its role in containerizing Go applications, enabling them to run anywhere with ease.

Why This Chapter Matters

As cloud computing becomes the norm for businesses and developers, knowing how to deploy and scale your Go applications is a critical skill. Understanding the tools and platforms that support cloud-native development, combined with Go's performance-oriented nature, will allow you to deliver robust and scalable applications that can handle large amounts of traffic.

This chapter will help you:

- Understand the benefits of cloud computing and why Go is well-suited for it.
- Learn how to deploy Go applications on cloud platforms like AWS, Google Cloud, and Heroku.
- Master the use of Docker for containerizing Go applications.
- Work through a hands-on project where you will deploy a Go application to the cloud using Docker and AWS.

Core Concepts and Theory

1. Introduction to Cloud Computing

Cloud computing is the delivery of computing services—servers, storage, databases, networking, software, and more—over the internet (the cloud). It allows businesses and developers to access technology resources on-demand without maintaining physical hardware.

Benefits of Cloud Computing

1. **Scalability**: Cloud services allow you to scale your application to meet demand without investing in physical infrastructure.
2. **Cost-Effectiveness**: With pay-as-you-go models, cloud computing reduces the need for upfront capital investment in hardware.
3. **High Availability**: Cloud platforms offer built-in redundancy and failover mechanisms, ensuring high availability of your services.
4. **Security**: Major cloud providers offer robust security features like encryption, multi-factor authentication, and compliance with industry standards.

5. **Flexibility**: Cloud services allow for the use of a wide variety of programming languages, frameworks, and technologies.

Go's Role in Cloud Computing

Go is well-suited for cloud applications due to its:

- **Concurrency**: Go's goroutines and channels allow for highly concurrent systems, ideal for cloud applications that need to handle many simultaneous tasks.
- **Simplicity**: Go's minimalistic design and ease of use make it ideal for rapid development and deployment in cloud environments.
- **Performance**: Go's compiled nature and efficient memory management enable it to handle high-throughput workloads often required in cloud applications.

2. Deploying Go Applications to the Cloud

Once you've developed a Go application, the next step is to deploy it to a cloud environment. Here, we will walk through deploying Go applications to some of the most popular cloud platforms: AWS, Google Cloud, and Heroku.

Deploying to AWS (Amazon Web Services)

AWS is one of the most widely used cloud platforms. Go applications can be deployed to AWS using services like EC2 (for virtual machines) or AWS Lambda (for serverless computing).

Steps for deploying a Go application to AWS EC2:

1. **Create an EC2 instance:** Log in to AWS and create an EC2 instance. Choose an

Ubuntu instance or any other Linux-based OS.

2. **Install Go**: SSH into your EC2 instance and install Go by running:

```bash
sudo apt update
sudo apt install golang-go
```

3. **Deploy your Go code:** Clone your Go project repository or upload your code to the EC2 instance.

4. **Run the application**: Navigate to your Go project directory and run the application:

```bash
go run main.go
```

5. **Open the security group:** Update the EC2 security group to allow inbound traffic on the port your Go application is running on (e.g., port 8080).

6. **Access your application:** Use the public IP of your EC2 instance to access your Go application.

Deploying to Google Cloud Platform (GCP)

Google Cloud provides services like Compute Engine (VMs) and Google Kubernetes Engine (GKE) for deploying Go applications.

Steps for deploying a Go application to GCP:

1. **Create a Google Cloud account:** Sign up or log in to Google Cloud Platform.
2. **Install Google Cloud SDK:** Install the Google Cloud SDK on your local machine:

```
bash

curl https://sdk.cloud.google.com |
bash
```

3. **Create a GCP instance**: Create a Compute Engine instance via the Google Cloud Console.

4. **Install Go on GCP**: SSH into your instance and install Go as you would on a regular Linux machine.

5. **Run your Go application**: Upload your application to the VM and run it using:

```bash
go run main.go
```

6. **Set up firewall rules**: Allow incoming traffic to the port your Go application is running on.

Deploying to Heroku

Heroku is a Platform-as-a-Service (PaaS) that simplifies the deployment of applications. It abstracts away infrastructure management and provides a streamlined way to deploy Go applications.

Steps for deploying a Go application to Heroku:

1. **Install Heroku CLI**: Download and install the Heroku CLI tool from Heroku's website.
2. **Create a Heroku app**: Log in to Heroku and create a new app:

```
bash

heroku create my-go-app
```

3. **Deploy your code**: Initialize a Git repository and push your Go code to Heroku:

```
bash

git init
git add .
git commit -m "Initial commit"
heroku git:remote -a my-go-app
```

```
git push heroku master
```

4. **Set up Go buildpack:** Heroku will automatically detect Go applications using the Go buildpack. If needed, you can configure the buildpack explicitly:

```bash
heroku buildpacks:set heroku/go
```

5. **Access your app:** Once deployed, Heroku will provide a URL where your Go app is accessible.

---

3. Using Go with Docker

Docker is a platform that enables developers to package applications and their dependencies into a standardized unit called a container. Docker containers ensure that your application runs consistently across different environments. For Go developers, Docker is an excellent tool for packaging Go applications and deploying them to the cloud.

What is Docker?

Docker provides a lightweight, portable environment for running applications. Containers can run on any machine that has Docker installed, which makes them perfect for deploying cloud-native applications.

Creating a Dockerfile for Go Applications

A **Dockerfile** is a text file that contains instructions to build a Docker image. Let's look at a simple Dockerfile for a Go application:

```
dockerfile

# Start from the official Go image
FROM golang:1.16-alpine

# Set the current working directory in
the container
```

```
WORKDIR /app

#  the Go source code into the
container
 . .

# Build the Go application
RUN go build -o main .

# Expose port 8080
EXPOSE 8080

# Run the Go application
CMD ["./main"]
```

This Dockerfile does the following:

1. **FROM golang:1.16-alpine**: Uses an official Go image based on Alpine Linux for a smaller image size.
2. **WORKDIR /app**: Sets the working directory inside the container to /app.

3. **. .**: Copies the local application files into the container.
4. **RUN go build -o main .**: Builds the Go application.
5. **EXPOSE 8080**: Exposes port 8080 (assuming the Go app listens on this port).
6. **CMD ["./main"]**: Runs the Go application when the container starts.

Building and Running a Docker Container

To build and run the Docker container for your Go application:

1. **Build the Docker image**:

```
bash

docker build -t my-go-app .
```

2. **Run the Docker container**:

```
bash
```

```
docker run -p 8080:8080 my-go-app
```

This will start the Go application inside a container and bind port 8080 on your local machine to port 8080 in the container.

Using Docker with Cloud Platforms

Once your Go application is containerized, you can easily deploy it to cloud platforms. For example:

- **AWS**: Use **Elastic Container Service (ECS)** or **Elastic Kubernetes Service (EKS)** to deploy your Dockerized Go application.
- **Google Cloud**: Deploy your Dockerized app to **Google Kubernetes Engine (GKE)** or use **Cloud Run** for serverless containers.
- **Heroku**: Deploy your Dockerized Go application to Heroku by pushing your Docker image directly.

Hands-on Examples & Projects

Building a Simple Blog Application Using Go and Docker

Now that we have covered the key concepts, let's build a simple **blog application**. In this hands-on project, you will create a RESTful API where users can create, read, update, and delete blog posts.

Step 1: Define the Post Model

Create a Post struct with the fields ID, Title, and Content:

```
go

package main

import "time"

type Post struct {
    ID        string    `json:"id"`
```

```
    Title   string    `json:"title"`
    Content string    `json:"content"`
    Created time.Time `json:"created"`
}
```

Step 2: Set Up the API Routes

You will use gorilla/mux to create the routes for handling CRUD operations:

```
go

package main

import (
    "encoding/json"
    "fmt"
    "net/http"
    "github.com/gorilla/mux"
)

var posts []Post

func getPosts(w http.ResponseWriter, r
*http.Request) {
    json.NewEncoder(w).Encode(posts)
```

```
}

func createPost(w http.ResponseWriter,
r *http.Request) {
    var post Post
    err :=
json.NewDecoder(r.Body).Decode(&post)
    if err != nil {
        http.Error(w, err.Error(),
http.StatusBadRequest)
        return
    }

    post.ID = fmt.Sprintf("%d",
len(posts)+1)
    post.Created = time.Now()
    posts = append(posts, post)
    w.WriteHeader(http.StatusCreated)
    json.NewEncoder(w).Encode(post)
}
```

Step 3: Create a Dockerfile

Use the Dockerfile discussed earlier to containerize the Go application.

Step 4: Build and Deploy the Application

1. Build the Docker image:

```bash
docker build -t my-blog-app .
```

2. Run the Docker container locally to test:

```bash
docker run -p 8080:8080 my-blog-app
```

3. Deploy the Docker container to **AWS**, **Google Cloud**, or **Heroku**, as previously explained.

Advanced Techniques & Optimization

Optimizing for High Availability

When deploying Go applications in the cloud, ensure high availability:

- **Load Balancing:** Use load balancers to distribute traffic across multiple instances of your application.
- **Auto-scaling:** Set up auto-scaling in cloud platforms like AWS or Google Cloud to automatically scale your application based on traffic demand.

Monitoring and Logging

Use cloud-native monitoring tools such as AWS CloudWatch or Google Cloud Monitoring to track the health of your application and set up alerts.

Troubleshooting and Problem-Solving

Common Issues

- **Database Connectivity:** Ensure your cloud database instance is accessible from your application. Double-check security groups or firewall rules.

- **Docker Image Issues:** If your Docker container fails to start, ensure the Go application is correctly built and the correct dependencies are included.
- **Scaling Problems:** If your application becomes slow under load, optimize database queries, use caching, and make use of Go's concurrency model.

Debugging Tips

- Use logging libraries like logrus or zap to help debug your cloud application.
- Monitor the cloud provider's logs for any errors related to networking or infrastructure.

Conclusion & Next Steps

In this chapter, you learned how to leverage Go for cloud computing. From deploying Go applications to AWS, Google Cloud, and Heroku, to containerizing them with Docker, you now have the knowledge to build scalable, cloud-native applications.

Next, explore more advanced topics such as serverless computing with Go and the use of Kubernetes for orchestration. Understanding how to build, deploy, and scale applications in the cloud is an essential skill in today's development environment.

Chapter 9: Debugging, Profiling, and Optimizing Your Go Code

Introduction

Writing code is only part of the journey in developing high-quality applications. The real challenge often comes when things don't work as expected. Debugging, profiling, and optimization are critical stages in the development process that can significantly improve the performance, memory usage, and reliability of your Go applications.

In this chapter, we will explore how to debug Go code efficiently, identify performance bottlenecks, and optimize your Go applications for better scalability and resource management.

Debugging and profiling are vital skills for developers, and understanding how to analyze and improve your code can make the difference between a mediocre app and a high-performance one.

You'll learn about Go's built-in debugging tools, such as **Delve**, and how to use them to troubleshoot issues in your code. We'll also dive into Go's **profiling tools**, such as pprof, to measure and optimize your application's performance. Finally, we'll look at best practices for **optimizing code**, improving memory management, and understanding Go's garbage collection to ensure efficient resource usage.

This chapter will also include a hands-on project where you'll refactor and optimize a previously built project, applying debugging and optimization techniques to enhance its performance.

What You Will Learn:

- **Debugging with Go**: Learn how to use the **Delve** debugger and best practices for troubleshooting Go applications.
- **Profiling**: Discover how to profile Go applications using **pprof** and identify performance bottlenecks.
- **Optimizing Code**: Identify inefficient code, optimize it, and manage memory usage effectively.
- **Hands-on Project**: Refactor and optimize a previously built Go application to improve performance and memory usage.

Core Concepts and Theory

1. Debugging with Go

Introduction to Debugging

Debugging is the process of finding and fixing bugs or issues in a program. Go provides several tools and practices that make debugging easier, ensuring that you can identify problems early in the development process.

Go's primary tool for debugging is **Delve**, a powerful debugger for Go applications. Delve allows you to step through your code, inspect variables, evaluate expressions, and track down issues in a more interactive way than traditional print-based debugging.

Using Delve for Debugging

Delve is an essential tool for Go developers. It provides an interactive shell where you can run your Go program, set breakpoints, step through code, inspect variables, and evaluate expressions.

Installing Delve

To install Delve, run the following command:

```bash
go install github.com/go-
delve/delve/cmd/dlv@latest
```

Once installed, you can use dlv to start debugging your Go application.

Basic Debugging with Delve

1. **Start Delve**: To start debugging your Go program with Delve, run:

```bash
dlv debug path/to/your/program.go
```

2. **Setting Breakpoints**: You can set a breakpoint at a specific line number or function:

```bash
break main.main
break 10  # Set a breakpoint at line 10
```

3. **Stepping Through Code**: You can step through your code one line at a time using the following commands:
   - next – Execute the next line of code.
   - step – Step into functions.
   - continue – Continue execution until the next breakpoint.
4. **Inspecting Variables**: While paused at a breakpoint, you can inspect the values of variables:

```bash
print myVariable
```

5. **Evaluating Expressions**: You can evaluate expressions in the current context:

```bash
eval 2 + 3
```

By using Delve, you can identify logical errors, inspect the state of variables, and step through your code to understand the flow of execution.

Best Practices for Debugging

- **Isolate the Issue**: Narrow down the problem area by commenting out unrelated code or adding print statements.
- **Reproduce the Error**: Try to recreate the error consistently to understand its conditions.
- **Use Logging**: Log messages can provide insights into your application's behavior. Libraries like logrus and zap provide structured logging that is more useful than simple fmt.Println() statements.

- **Test Edge Cases:** Always test edge cases and unexpected inputs to identify potential issues.

---

2. Profiling Go Applications

Introduction to Profiling

Profiling is the process of analyzing your program's behavior to find performance bottlenecks, excessive memory usage, or inefficient code paths. Go has excellent profiling tools built into its standard library, particularly **pprof**, which can be used to profile CPU and memory usage in real-time.

Profiling helps you understand how your application behaves during execution, which functions are consuming the most resources, and where optimizations are necessary.

Using pprof for Profiling

pprof is a Go package that allows you to capture and analyze performance data. You can profile CPU usage, memory allocation, and other statistics that help you understand your program's resource consumption.

Adding pprof to Your Application

To use pprof, you need to import the net/http/pprof package and start an HTTP server that exposes the profiling data.

Here's an example of setting up pprof:

```
go

import (
    "net/http"
    _ "net/http/pprof"  // Import pprof
package for side-effects
    "log"
    "net/http"
)
```

```
func main() {
    // Start pprof server in a separate
goroutine
    go func() {

log.Println(http.ListenAndServe("localh
ost:6060", nil))  // Default pprof port
    }()

    // Your application logic here
    // Example: an HTTP server
    http.HandleFunc("/", func(w
http.ResponseWriter, r *http.Request) {
        w.Write([]byte("Hello,
world!"))
    })

log.Fatal(http.ListenAndServe(":8080",
nil))
}
```

Capturing Profiling Data

Once the pprof server is running, you can access different types of profiling data:

- **CPU Profile**: Captures where your program is spending CPU time.
- **Heap Profile**: Shows memory allocation.
- **Goroutine Profile**: Shows the state of all goroutines.
- **Threadcreate Profile**: Provides information about threads.

For example, to capture a CPU profile, run the following command while your application is running:

```bash
go tool pprof
http://localhost:6060/debug/pprof/profi
le?seconds=30
```

This will capture 30 seconds of CPU profiling data, which you can analyze to understand performance issues.

Analyzing Profiling Data

Once you have captured profiling data, you can visualize it and identify performance bottlenecks. The pprof tool provides several ways to analyze the data, including:

- **Flame graphs**: These show which functions consume the most CPU time.
- **Memory allocation**: Understanding how much memory each part of your code allocates.

Example of starting a pprof session:

```
bash

go tool pprof
http://localhost:6060/debug/pprof/heap
```

Best Practices for Profiling

- **Profile in Production:** Set up profiling endpoints in production environments to monitor real-time performance.
- **Profile Over Time:** Regularly profile your application to track performance degradation.
- **Use Profiles for Bottleneck Identification:** Focus on optimizing the most resource-intensive parts of your application.

---

3. Optimizing Code

Identifying Inefficient Code

Code optimization is the process of improving your code to make it run faster or use fewer resources. It starts by identifying parts of your program that consume excessive CPU or memory.

Memory Management in Go

Go handles memory management through **garbage collection (GC)**, which automatically reclaims memory that is no longer in use. However, poor memory management can still lead to performance issues, such as excessive memory allocation or frequent garbage collection pauses.

To optimize memory usage:

- **Avoid unnecessary allocations**: Use memory-efficient data structures (e.g., arrays over slices when the size is fixed).
- **Reuse memory**: Reuse objects or buffers where possible to reduce the need for garbage collection.

- **Limit goroutine creation**: Creating too many goroutines can lead to high memory usage and performance degradation. Use worker pools or channels to manage goroutines.

Optimizing for Performance

Performance optimization often involves improving code execution speed or reducing resource consumption. Common strategies include:

- **Use efficient algorithms**: Always choose the most efficient algorithm for your task (e.g., sorting, searching).
- **Use concurrency effectively**: Go's goroutines and channels can be leveraged to improve parallelism and reduce execution time.

- **Profile before optimizing**: Before making optimizations, profile your code to ensure you are targeting the right areas.

Tools and Setup

Tools Required

- **Go Programming Language**: Ensure you have the latest version of Go installed.
- **Delve**: A debugger for Go. Install it using:

```bash
go install github.com/go-delve/delve/cmd/dlv@latest
```

- **pprof**: Go's built-in profiling tool. You can use it directly with the net/http/pprof package to profile your application.

Setting Up the Development Environment

1. **Install Go**: Install Go from the official Go website.
2. **Install Delve**: Follow the installation instructions provided earlier.
3. **Set Up Profiling**: Add the net/http/pprof import to your application to enable profiling.
4. **Run Your Application**: After setting up profiling, run your Go application and collect profiling data using the appropriate pprof commands.

Hands-on Examples & Projects

Refactoring and Optimizing a Go Application

In this hands-on project, we will refactor and optimize a simple Go application. Let's assume we previously built a blog API, and now we want to optimize its performance and memory usage.

1. **Step 1: Profile the Application** First, we profile the blog API to identify performance bottlenecks. Use the pprof tool to collect CPU and memory profiles.
2. **Step 2: Refactor Code** After analyzing the profiles, we identify inefficient code and memory leaks. Refactor the application by:
    - Replacing inefficient algorithms with more optimized ones.
    - Minimizing memory allocations.
3. **Step 3: Optimize Memory Usage** Optimize memory usage by reusing buffers and ensuring that large data structures are cleaned up properly.
4. **Step 4: Implement Concurrency** Use Go's goroutines and channels to improve

concurrency in parts of the application that handle multiple requests simultaneously.

Advanced Techniques & Optimization

Using Goroutines for Concurrency

Goroutines provide a way to execute functions concurrently, without the complexity of threads. Using goroutines and channels can significantly improve performance by processing tasks in parallel.

Garbage Collection Optimization

While Go's garbage collector is efficient, you can reduce its impact by:

- **Reducing allocations**: Minimize the creation of temporary objects that trigger garbage collection.

- **Using object pools**: The sync.Pool type can be used to reuse objects and reduce memory allocation overhead.

Troubleshooting and Problem-Solving

Common Challenges

- **Memory Leaks**: If your application consumes memory over time without releasing it, you may have a memory leak. Use pprof to identify where memory is being allocated.
- **Concurrency Issues**: Race conditions and deadlocks are common when working with concurrency. Use Go's race detector to identify race conditions in your code.

Troubleshooting Tips

- **Use Delve to Set Breakpoints**: Delve allows you to set breakpoints and step through code to understand where things are going wrong.
- **Profile Regularly**: Regular profiling ensures you identify and fix performance bottlenecks before they affect your users.

Conclusion & Next Steps

In this chapter, we learned how to debug, profile, and optimize Go applications. We used **Delve** for debugging, **pprof** for profiling, and explored several techniques to improve performance and memory usage. Additionally, we worked through a hands-on project where we refactored and optimized an application.

Next, consider exploring advanced topics such as building microservices with Go, integrating with databases, or using Go in distributed systems. By continuously profiling and optimizing your code, you'll be able to create fast, efficient, and scalable Go applications that can handle real-world challenges.

Keep practicing and applying the skills you've learned, and soon you'll be a Go optimization expert!

Conclusion: Taking Your Go Skills Further

Introduction

By now, you've journeyed through the fundamental concepts of Go programming, completed hands-on projects, and acquired a solid foundation in developing efficient, scalable, and maintainable applications. You've learned how to debug, profile, optimize, and deploy your Go applications to the cloud. More importantly, you've gained the confidence and technical knowledge to tackle Go-based challenges, whether you're working on professional projects or pursuing personal growth.

Go is a powerful language with an ever-growing ecosystem that has become a go-to tool for many developers and organizations. From building web servers and **APIs** to developing concurrent systems and cloud-native applications, Go has a place in almost every facet of modern software development.

But as you know, learning doesn't end with the basics. In this conclusion chapter, we will outline the next steps in your Go programming journey, suggest resources for continuing your learning, and explore advanced topics you can delve into. We'll also discuss how you can get involved in the Go community and contribute to open-source projects, which will not only help you improve your Go skills but also expand your professional network.

What You Will Learn:

- **Next Steps**: Where to go from here to deepen your Go knowledge.

- **Resources:** Books, websites, and tools to continue learning.
- **Community Engagement:** How to get involved with the Go community and contribute to open-source projects.
- **Challenge Yourself:** Ways to challenge yourself and improve your Go skills through side projects and advanced topics.

This chapter will serve as your guide to the next steps, helping you take your Go skills further and integrate them into real-world challenges.

Core Concepts and Theory

1. Next Steps for Go Programming

As a Go programmer, you now have the fundamental knowledge to write Go applications and troubleshoot, optimize, and deploy them.

However, there is always more to learn. To truly excel with Go, it's essential to keep building on what you've already learned and to start exploring more advanced topics. Here are some next steps that can deepen your understanding and proficiency in Go.

Explore Advanced Go Features

1. **Concurrency in Depth:** Go's concurrency model is one of its most powerful features. You've already touched on goroutines and channels, but there are more advanced concurrency patterns you can explore, such as worker pools, fan-in/fan-out, and message queues. Understanding how to leverage Go's concurrency model at scale can dramatically improve your applications' performance and responsiveness.

2. **Error Handling Best Practices**: While Go's error handling is simple, it's not always intuitive. Delve deeper into best practices for error handling in Go, including wrapping errors with more context and using custom error types to improve readability and maintainability.

3. **Design Patterns**: Go doesn't enforce object-oriented principles, but you can still apply various design patterns (such as Singleton, Factory, and Observer) to build more maintainable and scalable systems. Understanding these patterns and knowing how to apply them effectively will make you a better Go programmer.

Learn Go's Ecosystem

Go's ecosystem includes a wide range of third-party libraries and frameworks that can help you build more sophisticated applications. Explore the following areas:

- **Web Frameworks**: Although Go's net/http package is powerful, frameworks like **Gin**, **Echo**, and **Beego** offer additional features and can help speed up development.
- **Database Libraries**: Learn how to use **GORM**, **sqlx**, or other libraries to simplify database interactions in Go.
- **Microservices**: Go is an excellent choice for building microservices. Explore tools like **Go-kit** and **gRPC** for building distributed systems.
- **Testing**: Understanding Go's testing framework and incorporating unit tests into your workflow is crucial for ensuring the reliability of your applications.

2. Resources for Continuing Your Go Learning Journey

While this chapter has covered many essential topics, the Go ecosystem is vast, and continuous learning is key to becoming an expert. Here are some recommended resources to continue your Go programming journey.

Books

1. **"The Go Programming Language" by Alan A. A. Donovan and Brian W. Kernighan**: This is the definitive book for learning Go. It covers all of Go's features in depth and is suitable for beginners as well as experienced developers.
2. **"Go in Action" by William Kennedy**: A practical guide to Go programming, with plenty of hands-on examples and best practices for Go application development.

3. **"Go Web Programming" by Sau Sheong Chang:** If you're interested in web development with Go, this book is an excellent resource that covers everything from building APIs to deploying web applications in the cloud.

Websites and Tutorials

1. **Go Documentation:** The official Go documentation is always the best place to find up-to-date, authoritative information about Go.

2. **Go Wiki**: The Go Wiki on GitHub offers in-depth guides and tutorials on advanced Go topics, including concurrency patterns, error handling, and more.

3. **Go by Example**: Go by Example is a fantastic resource for learning Go through practical examples.

4. **Exercism**: The Exercism Go track is an interactive platform where you can practice Go through coding exercises and get feedback from mentors.

Courses and Video Tutorials

1. **Go in Action (Pluralsight)**: This course takes you from beginner to intermediate Go programming with real-world examples and challenges.

2. **Go Programming (Udemy)**: A popular Go course on Udemy that covers everything from Go basics to more advanced topics like concurrency and testing.

3. **Go on YouTube**: YouTube has many high-quality tutorials and conferences that cover Go programming, including talks from the Go community and organizations that use Go at scale.

---

3. How to Get Involved in the Go Community

One of the most rewarding aspects of being a Go developer is the vibrant, welcoming community. By contributing to the community, you not only help others but also learn new techniques, get feedback on your code, and keep up with the latest trends.

Contribute to Open Source

Go has a thriving open-source ecosystem, and there are plenty of opportunities for developers to contribute. Some ways to get involved:

- **Go Core**: Contribute to Go itself by fixing bugs, improving documentation, or adding features.

- **Third-Party Libraries**: Many libraries and frameworks built on top of Go are open-source. Contribute by reporting issues, submitting bug fixes, or adding new features.
- **Create Your Own Projects**: Don't just contribute to others' projects—create your own. Building your own Go-based open-source project is a great way to give back to the community and showcase your skills.

Join Go Meetups and Conferences

- **Go Developer Meetups**: Many cities have Go user groups that meet regularly to discuss Go programming, share knowledge, and network. Check out Meetup.com to find local Go groups.
- **Go Conferences**: Attend conferences such as **GopherCon** to meet other Go

developers, listen to talks from industry experts, and stay updated on the latest trends in Go development.

Online Communities

- **Go Reddit**: The Go subreddit is an excellent place to ask questions, share knowledge, and discuss Go-related topics.
- **Go Slack**: Join the official Golang Slack to communicate with other Go developers, ask questions, and share your projects.
- **Go Discord**: Many Go developers also hang out on Discord. You can find Go-related servers where you can ask questions and participate in discussions.

4. Challenge Yourself

The best way to improve as a Go developer is to challenge yourself through side projects and continuous learning. Here are some ways you can do this:

Start Your Own Projects

Building your own projects is one of the best ways to solidify your understanding of Go. Whether it's a web application, a RESTful API, or a command-line tool, creating something from scratch forces you to apply everything you've learned. Here are some ideas:

- **Build a personal website or blog** using Go's net/http package or a framework like Gin.
- **Develop a to-do app** with Go and integrate it with a database like PostgreSQL.

- **Create a REST API** that can handle various operations (CRUD) and use Go's concurrency to handle high loads.

Explore Advanced Topics

- **Machine Learning with Go**: While Go is not traditionally associated with machine learning, you can still explore libraries like **Gorgonia** and **Golearn** to dive into machine learning and neural networks with Go.
- **Blockchain Development**: Go is widely used in the blockchain space. Explore Go libraries such as **Go-Ethereum** to understand how to build decentralized applications (dApps).
- **Cloud-Native Development**: As you've learned in previous chapters, Go is ideal for cloud-native applications. Explore

Kubernetes, Docker, and cloud platforms like AWS and GCP to build scalable, cloud-based systems.

- **Distributed Systems:** Learn about building distributed systems using Go, including message queues, microservices, and tools like gRPC.

Join Competitions and Coding Challenges

Participating in coding competitions can also help you improve your Go skills:

- **LeetCode** and **HackerRank** have Go as one of their supported languages for coding challenges.
- **Advent of Code** is a yearly event where programmers solve small puzzles every day. It's a fun way to improve problem-solving skills in Go.

Conclusion & Next Steps

Congratulations on making it through this comprehensive Go programming journey! You've acquired essential skills and gained hands-on experience in building Go applications, optimizing them for performance, and deploying them to the cloud. You've learned how to debug your applications, profile performance, and get involved in the Go community.

Next Steps

- Dive deeper into advanced Go topics, including concurrency patterns, Go microservices, or blockchain development.
- Continue building projects and contribute to open-source Go libraries.
- Participate in Go meetups, conferences, and online communities to stay connected and keep learning.

By challenging yourself and applying your Go knowledge in real-world projects, you'll continue to grow as a Go developer. Keep coding, keep learning, and never stop exploring the endless possibilities with Go!

Appendix: Go Resources and Tools

As you continue your Go journey, it's important to have access to the right resources and tools that can support and accelerate your development process. In this appendix, we will explore the official Go documentation, best practices, some essential libraries and frameworks that will aid your development, and how to get involved with the Go community through meetups and other community resources.

Go Documentation and Best Practices

1. Official Go Documentation

The official Go documentation is your primary resource for understanding the Go language. It provides in-depth explanations of all the language features, the Go runtime, and the standard library. If you ever need clarification on Go's behavior or a specific function, the documentation is a great place to start.

- **Go Language Specification:** https://golang.org/ref/spec
  This is the definitive specification of the Go programming language, detailing its syntax, semantics, and standard library. This is a great reference if you need to dive deep into the formal aspects of Go.
- **Go Wiki:** https://github.com/golang/go/wiki
  This is an unofficial resource hosted on GitHub. It provides helpful guides on setting up Go, building projects, and even tips on writing idiomatic Go code.
- **Go By Example:** https://gobyexample.com/

This website offers practical examples that illustrate how to use Go constructs. It's perfect for learners who prefer hands-on examples and need to see real code in action.

- **Go Doc:** https://pkg.go.dev/golang.org/x/tools/cmd/godoc
  Godoc provides a web-based interface for exploring Go documentation. You can use it to explore libraries, functions, and other code elements.

2. Go Best Practices

Following best practices in Go can make your code cleaner, more efficient, and easier to maintain. Here are some best practices that will help you write better Go code:

- **Use Idiomatic Go**: Go has a strong emphasis on writing idiomatic code, which can often be different from other languages you may have used. Always prefer simplicity and clarity over complexity. Go's standard library is an excellent example of idiomatic code.
- **Error Handling**: Go doesn't use exceptions; instead, it relies on explicit error checking. Always check for errors after performing an operation that can fail. Handle errors as close to the source as possible.
- **Avoid Global State**: Keep your functions pure, meaning they should not depend on or modify global state. If your function requires access to a global state, pass that state as a parameter instead.

- **Use Goroutines and Channels for Concurrency**: Go's concurrency model is one of its strongest features. When writing concurrent applications, make use of goroutines and channels to avoid thread management issues and race conditions.
- **Keep Functions Small and Focused**: A good function should do one thing and do it well. Break your logic into small, reusable functions to improve readability and maintainability.

Recommended Libraries and Frameworks for Go Developers

One of the best things about Go is the wide range of third-party libraries and frameworks available for developers. These libraries can significantly speed up development, simplify your code, and enhance your application's functionality. Below is a list of some essential libraries and frameworks you should consider as a Go developer.

1. Web Frameworks

Although Go's built-in net/http package is quite powerful for web development, some frameworks add additional features that make development faster and easier.

- **Gin**: https://github.com/gin-gonic/gin Gin is one of the most popular web frameworks for Go, known for its high performance and minimalist design. It offers routing, middleware support, JSON validation, and more.
- **Echo**: https://github.com/labstack/echo Echo is another fast and extensible web framework for Go. It focuses on providing a minimal API and is particularly useful

when building RESTful APIs and microservices.

- **Beego**: https://github.com/astaxie/beego Beego is a full-fledged MVC framework for Go. It comes with built-in support for routing, ORM, session management, and more. It's a good choice if you want to build more traditional web applications.

2. Database Libraries

Go supports a wide range of databases. To make working with them easier, several libraries are available to simplify database interactions.

- **GORM**: https://gorm.io/ GORM is a full-featured ORM (Object-Relational Mapping) library for Go. It makes it easier to interact with databases by providing features like migrations, relationships, and query building.

- **sqlx:** https://github.com/jmoiron/sqlx sqlx is an extension to the standard Go database/sql package that provides additional functionality such as named query support, scanning rows into structs, and more.
- **pgx:** https://github.com/jackc/pgx pgx is a PostgreSQL driver and toolkit for Go. It provides advanced features and is optimized for performance, making it a great choice if you're working specifically with PostgreSQL databases.

3. Testing Libraries

Testing is an essential part of writing Go code. Fortunately, Go has a built-in testing framework, but there are also many third-party libraries to enhance your testing process.

- **Testify:** https://github.com/stretchr/testify
  Testify is a toolkit for testing in Go. It offers helpful features like assertions, mock objects, and test suites, making it easier to write unit tests.
- **GoMock:** https://github.com/golang/mock
  GoMock is a mock object library for Go, making it easier to mock interfaces for unit testing.
- **Gocheck:** https://github.com/go-check/check
  Gocheck is another testing framework that offers advanced features like setup and teardown methods and test suites, making it an excellent choice for testing larger Go applications.

4. Concurrency and Parallelism

Go's concurrency model is one of its most powerful features. Here are some libraries that help you harness the power of concurrency and parallelism in Go.

- **goroutines**: While Go's standard library is sufficient for most concurrency tasks, you can use packages like goroutines for simplified concurrency management.
    - **Go Worker Pool:** https://github.com/gammazero/workerpool
      This is a lightweight Go worker pool library that helps you manage concurrent work efficiently.

5. Authentication and Authorization

If you're building web applications or APIs, you'll need to handle user authentication and authorization. These libraries can simplify the process.

- **OAuth2:** https://github.com/golang/oauth2
  The OAuth2 package from the Go standard library provides support for working with OAuth2, which is widely used for user authentication.
- **JWT-go:** https://github.com/dgrijalva/jwt-go
  JWT (JSON Web Token) is commonly used for authenticating users. JWT-go is a library for encoding and decoding JWTs in Go.

Community Resources and Go Meetups

1. Go Community Resources

Getting involved with the Go community is one of the best ways to keep learning and stay up-to-date with new developments in the Go ecosystem. Here are some excellent resources for connecting with other Go developers:

- **Go Forum:** https://forum.golang.org/ The Go Forum is a place where Go developers can ask questions, share knowledge, and discuss Go-related topics.
- **Go Wiki:** https://github.com/golang/go/wiki The Go Wiki on GitHub has a wealth of information, including guides, best practices, and tools for Go developers.
- **Go Documentation:** https://golang.org/doc/ The official Go documentation contains tutorials, language specifications, and examples, and it's the most authoritative resource available.

- **Slack Channel:** https://invite.slack.golangbridge.org/
  Join the Go Slack workspace to ask questions, share your projects, and collaborate with other developers in real-time.

2. Go Meetups and Conferences

Joining local meetups or attending conferences can provide excellent networking opportunities and a chance to learn from others. Here are a few ways to get involved:

- **Meetup.com**: Search for Go meetups in your area on Meetup.com. These are great opportunities to meet like-minded developers and discuss Go-related topics.
- **GopherCon**: https://www.gophercon.com/
  GopherCon is the annual Go conference where developers from all over the world

gather to learn, share ideas, and network. It's one of the best events for Go developers to stay updated on the latest Go trends.

- **GoBridge**: https://golangbridge.org/ GoBridge is a nonprofit organization focused on building a diverse Go community. They offer resources, mentoring, and community events.

---

3. Online Communities

In addition to local meetups, there are several online communities where Go developers can interact, collaborate, and share knowledge:

- **Go Subreddit**: https://www.reddit.com/r/golang/ The Go subreddit is an excellent place for discussions, news, and learning resources about Go. It's one of the largest online communities dedicated to Go programming.

- **Stack Overflow:** https://stackoverflow.com/questions/tagged/go
  The Go tag on Stack Overflow is a great resource for asking and answering questions related to Go development.
- **Go Discord Server**: Many Go developers interact on various Go-specific Discord servers. Search for Go-related communities on Discord where you can collaborate and get advice.

Conclusion

Now that you've explored Go documentation, libraries, and frameworks, as well as resources for connecting with the Go community, you're well-equipped to continue learning and improving your Go skills. The Go ecosystem is vibrant and growing, with numerous opportunities for you to engage, contribute, and learn.

Whether you're building your own side projects, contributing to open-source initiatives, or diving deeper into advanced topics like machine learning, Go will continue to be a valuable tool in your developer toolkit. Keep exploring, keep building, and, most importantly, enjoy the journey as you expand your expertise in Go!

www.ingramcontent.com/pod-product-compliance
Lightning Source LLC
LaVergne TN
LVHW022339060326
832902LV00022B/4123
* 9 7 9 8 3 1 6 4 1 1 2 5 2 *